P9-DNR-598

Options
for Improving the Care of
Neglected and
Dependent
Children

**Program
Analysis
Applied to
Local
Government**

Marvin R. Burt
Louis H. Blair

Options
for Improving the Care of
Neglected and
Dependent
Children

Program Analysis Applied to Local Government

Marvin R. Burt
Louis H. Blair

In Cooperation With

The Metropolitan Government of Nashville
  and Davidson County
The Council of State Governments
The International City Management Association
The National Association of Counties
The National Governors' Conference
The National League of Cities
The United States Conference of Mayors

The Urban Institute
Washington, D.C.

March 1971

The work forming the basis for this publication was conducted
pursuant to a contract with the Department of Housing and
Urban Development. The views expressed are those of the authors
and do not necessarily represent the views of The Urban Institute
or the Department of Housing and Urban Development.

ISBN No. 87766-016-6
Library of Congress Catalog Card No. 71-161200
UI 73-108-74   May 1971

Available from:

Publications Office
The Urban Institute
2100 M Street, N. W.
Washington, D. C. 20037

List price: $2.75

Printed in the United States of America

Metropolitan Government of Nashville and Davidson County

OFFICE OF THE MAYOR
107 COURTHOUSE
NASHVILLE, TENNESSEE 37201

Foreword

We are increasingly concerned with problems of young people and Nashville-Davidson County is attempting to solve some of them.

During 1970, a consortium was brought together to find ways to improve the care of neglected and dependent children. They formed a joint study group consisting of representatives of the Metropolitan Government of Nashville and Davidson County and The Urban Institute. The State of Tennessee and the U. S. Department of Health, Education and Welfare and concerned voluntary agencies also provided valuable assistance. The participants, after an in-depth study, have presented both an evaluation of the shortcomings of the existing system as well as estimates of the costs and effectiveness of various options to improve it.

As a direct result of this effort, a new system for neglected and dependent children is now being actively developed. Depending upon the availability of funds, I have directed that proposed changes be implemented as rapidly as possible. Although it is frequently asked, who cares about neglected and dependent children, we will demonstrate that indeed we do care about the welfare of these children.

Since many of the difficulties in dealing with neglected and dependent children in Nashville-Davidson County are shared by other communities, we hope this study also will be interesting and instructive to others.

For instance, it may be pointed out that the study's approach to analyzing local government problems is all too rare today. Rather than examining bits and pieces of the child care system, it takes account of all the major components. And the study utilized systematic, thorough methods to highlight not only the immediate consequences but also impacts on future years of a variety of proposals. In short, we hope the study will help improve child care in Nashville-Davidson County and many other communities.

Mayor Beverly Briley
February 1971

Preface

This study has two major purposes: (1) to improve the care of neglected and dependent children in Nashville and Davidson County, Tennessee,
and (2) to develop and demonstrate improved methods by which local governments generally can analyze their programs and policies.

Not only persons throughout the country who are primarily involved in
child welfare, but also government managers who have general decision-
making responsibilities may find the conclusions and analytical methods
of value.

The approach in this study has a number of characteristics that are
seldom found in local government analyses. Among these are the following:

1. Most significantly, the components of the child care system in
Nashville were analyzed in the perspective of an overall system. The ana-
lysts did not examine piecemeal the actions of the Juvenile Court, the
Metropolitan Children's Home, various types of foster homes, various emergency services, the state welfare agency, the police department, and so
forth. Instead they tried to view all components as part of a balanced
system.

2. The analysis explicitly identifies the public objectives of the
system, selects specific evaluation criteria by which these objectives
might be measured, and attempts to provide these measurements.

3. The flow of neglected and dependent children has been examined
systematically--quantitatively and in detail--with particular attention
to the reasons that children enter the system and both the immediate and
long-term dispositions of their cases. A major and unusual characteristic
of this effort was the linking of the information on the records of individual neglected-dependent children from such agencies as the Juvenile
Court, the Metropolitan Children's Home, and the Tennessee Department of
Public Welfare (Davidson County Office). In addition, the information
system developed will permit ongoing periodic evaluation by the city for
future evaluation of the child care system.

4. A number of alternative programs are identified and different
combinations of these programs are explicitly examined as to their costs
and effectiveness. Possible funding options for the alternatives are also
identified. The analysis includes future-year implications, going beyond
the common practice of discussing only the first budget year. The analysis
presents and evaluates various options but leaves the decisions about the
"optimum" program to the political decision makers.

None of the techniques and methods used are esoteric or require very specialized technical know-how (except, perhaps, for the data processing elements which are available in most governments). The systematic, or "scientific," approach used may be unfamiliar to many local governments, but the methods are hardly beyond their reach. Some governments already have personnel with the backgrounds and talents to undertake similar studies, requiring only a minimum of guidance or examples such as this study. Other governments may need to obtain staff to undertake such analyses.

The main question is whether governments are willing to apply the needed resources for such studies. Local governments are attracted to the notion of applying all available resources to the action aspects of their programs, which appear already under-funded, leaving little or no money for analysis and evaluation. Approximately two man-years of effort were spent on this study, including part-time help. Much of this was devoted to collecting data. Follow-on studies in Nashville-Davidson on this topic can build on this data without repeating all the steps.

Yet without studies of this nature the government becomes committed to a continuation, year after year after year, to past methods of dealing with Nashville children. The current mix of programs was found to be wasteful of community resources and the source of unnecessary harm to the children. To stress the importance of analysis and evaluation, of course, is not to claim that all studies will necessarily be successful in pointing to dramatic improvements. But the potential is substantial.

The federal and state governments should encourage such studies by their own example, which only now are they beginning to do, as well as through legislation, funding support and technical assistance. As studies increase in quantity and quality, improved communication mechanisms should be devised so that significant findings can be made available promptly throughout the country. This would permit other governments to avoid "reinventing the wheel" and to concentrate on more advanced analytical efforts.

One final comment. The question has often been raised as to whether systematic analysis can be applied to the "human resource" areas of government and not only to the more hardware oriented programs. This study indicates that indeed much can be accomplished even in this difficult-to-quantify area.

Harry Hatry
Director of State-Local
Government Research Program
The Urban Institute

Robert Horton
Fiscal Administrative Assistant to the Mayor
Metropolitan Government of Nashville and
Davidson County

Acknowledgments

This study would not have been possible without the active cooperation and participation of many people. Professionals and volunteers alike helped surmount numerous obstacles and were highly motivated to do whatever could be done to improve the welfare of the neglected and dependent children.

The assistance of the Nashville Urban Observatory in this project is appreciated. Nashville is one of the 10 cities in this national program, supported by the Department of Housing and Urban Development and the U. S. Office of Education, aimed at linking cities and universities in the solution of urban problems.

Mr. Robert Horton, Assistant to the Mayor of Nashville-Davidson for Fiscal Affairs, contributed invaluable interest, active participation, and continued support. Mrs. Catherine Mates of the Urban Observatory and Peabody College demonstrated unusual initiative in the data-gathering effort. Special thanks are due to Judge R. W. Jenkins of the Davidson County Juvenile Court, Mrs. Jeanne Bowman, of the Tennessee Department of Public Welfare, and Mr. Ralph Baugh, of the Metropolitan Social Service Commission.

Funds for this study, provided by the U.S. Department of Housing and Urban Development and the Metropolitan Government of Nashville and Davidson County, are gratefully acknowledged.

A previous draft was reviewed by Worth Bateman, Donald Fisk, Harry Hatry, Joseph Lewis, and Kenneth Webb of the Urban Institute. Nashville project participants who reviewed the previous draft were: Ralph Baugh, Edward Binkley, Jeanne Bowman, George Currey, Virginia Dobbs, Clark Harris, Robert Horton, Richard Irvine, the Honorable Richard Jenkins, Patricia Lockett, William Moynihan, Elise Oliver, George Podelco, and Edward Sterling. HEW (Office of Child Development) reviewers were Beatrice Garrett and Ursula Gallagher.

The persons whose names appear below participated actively in this study. Project Team members actually worked on data gathering and analysis. The other participants provided data, information and insights into the various programs and agencies concerned with neglected and dependent children.

Project Team

Dr. Marvin R. Burt, Project Director, The Urban Institute
Mr. Louis Blair, The Urban Institute
Miss Rhona Pavis, The Urban Institute
Mr. George Podelco, Office of the Metropolitan Mayor and the Urban
    Observatory
Mr. Edward Sterling, MSW, Metropolitan Social Service Commission
Mr. David Johnson, Metropolitan Department of Finance, Data Processing
    Division

Mr. Tom Sparks, Metropolitan Department of Finance, Budget Division
Mrs. Catherine Mates, The Urban Observatory and Peabody College
Mrs. Elizabeth Fox, The Urban Observatory
Mr. William Gray, The Urban Observatory
Mr. Binod Karr, the Urban Observatory and Peabody College

Metropolitan Government of Nashville and Davidson County

Office of the Mayor

Mr. Robert Horton, Fiscal Assistant to the Mayor

Metropolitan Social Service Commission

Mrs. Camilla Caldwell, ACSW, Director
Mr. Ralph Baugh, Director, Metropolitan Richland Village
Mr. Bob McKissick, Assistant Director, Metropolitan Richland Village
Mrs. Jane Ambrose, Social Worker II

Metropolitan Juvenile Court

The Honorable Richard W. Jenkins, Juvenile Court Judge
Mr. Clark Harris, Chief Probation Officer
Mrs. Martha Marsh, MSW, Principal Probation Officer
Mrs. Christine Brown, MSW, Principal Probation Officer
Mr. Elston Winters, MSW, Supervising Probation Officer
Mrs. Beverly Hathcock, Intermediate Clerk

Metropolitan Police Department

Mr. Richard Irvine, Business Manager
Mr. George Currey, Commander, Youth Guidance Division

Metropolitan Board of Education

Dr. Virgina Dobbs, Director, Pupil Placement Service
Dr. Edward Binkley, Director, Educational Research

State of Tennessee

Department of Public Welfare

Mr. Herman Yeatman, MSW, Tennessee State Commissioner of Public Welfare
Mrs. Elise Oliver, MCSW, County Director
Mrs. Jeanne Bowman, MCSW, Field Supervisor III
Mrs. Patricia Lockett, Field Supervisor II
Miss Patricia O'Neil, MSW, Field Supervisor II
Mrs. Louise Green, Stenographer I

State Board of Education

Mr. Charles E. Barham, Superintendent, Tennessee Preparatory School

Voluntary Agencies

Madison Children's Home

Mr. Carl H. Kingsbury, MSW, Director of Social Service
Mrs. Shirley Campbell, Caseworker

Saint Mary Villa

Sister Mary Joyce, Administrator
Mrs. Roberta B. Jones, Caseworker

Tennessee Orphan Home

Mr. E. R. Moore, Superintendent

AGAPE

Mr. Howard Justiss, Director

U.S. Government

Department of Health, Education, and Welfare

Miss Beatrice L. Garrett, MSW, Specialist on Foster Family Care,
    Children's Bureau, Office of Child Development
Miss Ursula M. Gallagher, MSSA, Specialist on Adoptions and Services
    to Unmarried Parents, Children's Bureau, Office of Child Develop-
    ment

National Institutes of Mental Health

Dr. Wilbur Lewis

Cover photo by George de Vincent.

Contents

CHAPTER   PAGE

FOREWORD   5

PREFACE   7

ACKNOWLEDGMENTS   9

SUMMARY   19

NATIONAL RECOMMENDATIONS   26

I.   INTRODUCTION   29

II.   DESCRIPTION OF THE PRESENT SYSTEM   32

     How Children Enter the System
     Disposition of Children
     Richland Village

III.   OBJECTIVES AND EVALUATION CRITERIA   39

     Objectives
     Evaluation Criteria

IV.   INTAKE AND EMERGENCY CARE   42

     Revise Juvenile Court Intake Screening Procedures
     Emergency Caretaker Services
     Emergency Foster Homes
     Homemaker Service
     Alternative Program Combinations

V.   FINANCING INTAKE AND EMERGENCY CARE   68

VI.   LONGER-TERM CARE   75

     Possible Options for Improvement
     Lowering the Case Loads of Those Carrying Out
       Intensive Supervision
     Expanding Temporary and Permanent Foster Homes
     Creating Assembled Families' Home
     Subsidizing Adoptions
     Using Richland Village as a Residential Treatment
       Center

VII.   RECOMMENDATIONS   95

CONTENTS (continued)

APPENDIX   PAGE

A   ESTIMATING THE UNIVERSE OF NEED OF NEGLECTED AND   101
        DEPENDENT CHILDREN FOR AVAILABLE SERVICES

B   FINDINGS OF THE JOINT COMMISSION ON MENTAL HEALTH OF   104
        CHILDREN

C   DEPARTMENT OF PUBLIC WELFARE PROTECTIVE SERVICES   *
        REFERRALS

D   DATA SYSTEM   108

E   RICHLAND VILLAGE COST ANALYSIS   119

F   ADMINISTRATION OF JUSTICE PLANNING AGENCY PROGRAM   *
        DESCRIPTION

G   ANALYSIS OF THE EXISTING SYSTEM   *

H   METHODOLOGY   128

I   A PROPOSED CHILD WELFARE SYSTEM FOR PREVENTING AND   130
        HANDLING ABUSE, DEPENDENCY, AND NEGLECT COMPLAINTS

J   CALCULATION OF HOMEMAKER REQUIREMENTS   134

*   Starred items submitted to Nashville-Davidson; not included here
    but available on request from Urban Institute.

15

Figures

NUMBER		PAGE
II-1	FLOW OF CHILDREN THROUGH NEGLECTED AND DEPENDENT SYSTEM, 1969	33
IV-1	EMERGENCY FOSTER HOMES REQUIRED	54
IV-2	CHILDREN AND FAMILIES SERVED BY HOMEMAKERS	59
D-1	JUVENILE COURT AND DPW COMBINED RECORDING FORM	117
I-1	CHILD WELFARE SYSTEM FOR HANDLING ABUSE, DEPENDENCY, AND NEGLECT COMPLAINTS	132
J-1	DATE OF ENTRY AND LENGTH OF STAY OF FAMILY CASES AT RICHLAND VILLAGE, ILLUSTRATIVE EXAMPLE	135
J-2	NUMBER OF FAMILIES SERVED BY HOMEMAKERS, ILLUSTRATIVE EXAMPLE	136

Tables

NUMBER   PAGE

I-1   INTAKE AND EMERGENCY CARE -- ALTERNATIVE PROGRAM   22
       COMBINATIONS

I-2   EFFECTIVENESS AND COSTS OF SHORT-TERM ALTERNATIVES   24

II-1   N&D PETITIONS FILED DURING 1969 - BY REASON   33

II-2   N&D CHILDREN IN 1969 WITH DELINQUENCY RECORDS -- BY AGE   36

II-3   SUMMARY OF CHARACTERISTICS OF CHILDREN AT RICHLAND VILLAGE   37

IV-1   DESTINATION OF CHILDREN TEMPORARILY PLACED AT RICHLAND   44
       VILLAGE BY JUVENILE COURT IN 1969

IV-2   FAMILIES WITH N&D CHILDREN PLACED BY JUVENILE COURT   47
       INTAKE OFFICE - 1969

IV-3   24-HOUR SCREENING COSTS   50

IV-4   ANNUAL EMERGENCY FOSTER HOME COSTS   53

IV-5   JUVENILE COURT PLACEMENTS IN RICHLAND VILLAGE BY   56
       SELECTED REASON FOR ENTRY AND DISPOSITION - 1969

IV-6   ANNUAL COST PER HOMEMAKER   58

IV-7   DIFFERENT MIXES OF HOMEMAKERS   61

IV-8   TRADE-OFF BETWEEN 24-HOUR HOMEMAKER AND EMERGENCY   62
       FOSTER HOMES

IV-9   ALTERNATIVE MIX OF 24-HOUR HOMEMAKERS AND EMERGENCY   63
       FOSTER HOMES

IV-10 COSTS AND CHILDREN SERVED IN FOUR SHORT-TERM PROGRAM   64
       COMBINATIONS

IV-11 EFFECTIVENESS AND COSTS OF SHORT-TERM ALTERNATIVES   66

V-1   FINANCING ALTERNATIVES -- SHORT-TERM   70

V-2   RICHLAND VILLAGE FINANCING -- PUBLIC VS. PRIVATE   71
       INSTITUTION

TABLES (continued)

NUMBER		PAGE
V-3	RICHLAND VILLAGE FINANCING -- FAP AND LEAA	72
V-4	NET STATE AND LOCAL COSTS (Change from the Base)	74
VI-1	INTENSIVE SUPERVISION CASES - January 1, 1969-June 30, 1970	77
VI-2	CHILDREN PLACED WITH PARENT(S) OR RELATIVES January 1-June 30, 1969	79
VI-3	DPW FOSTER HOMES -- FOR BOTH N&D AND VOLUNTARY CASES July 1, 1969-September 30, 1970	81
VI-4	DEPARTMENT OF PUBLIC WELFARE FOSTER HOME PROGRAM -- N&D CASES ONLY	82
VI-5	DEPARTMENT OF PUBLIC WELFARE FOSTER HOME PROGRAM	84
VI-6	FOSTER HOME COSTS (Fiscal Year 1969-70)	85
VI-7	CHILD/MONTHS OF FOSTER CARE AND COSTS FOR A FIVE-YEAR PERMANENT FOSTER HOME PROGRAM	86
VI-8	PROGRAM LEVELS - LONGER-TERM	92
VI-9	FINANCING ALTERNATIVES -- LONGER-TERM	93
D-1	JUVENILE COURT CODING SHEET (For N&D and for Delinquency Petitions)	110
D-2	DEPARTMENT OF PUBLIC WELFARE CODING SHEET	113
D-3	BOARD OF EDUCATION CODING SHEET	115
E-1	CHILDREN AT RICHLAND VILLAGE - January 1, 1968 - April 20, 1970	120
E-2	CHILD-YEARS OF CARE AT RICHLAND VILLAGE	121
E-3	RICHLAND VILLAGE -- STAFF	122
E-4	RICHLAND VILLAGE STAFFING -- SEMI-VARIABLE	124

..

TABLES (continued)

NUMBER

PAGE

E-5   RICHLAND VILLAGE: COST BY CLASSIFICATION/OBJECT CODE --   125
        FISCAL YEAR 1969-1970

E-6   SEMI-VARIABLE COST ($000)
                                        126

E-7   METROPOLITAN CHILDREN'S HOME
        ANNUAL OPERATING COST AT ALTERNATIVE LOADS ($000)   127

Summary

SCOPE

The principal purpose of this study was to develop programs to improve the well-being of neglected and dependent children. It deals specifically with those children on whom neglect and dependency petitions have been filed with the Juvenile Court of Metropolitan Nashville-Davidson County, Tennessee. A joint Metro-Urban Institute team analyzed the effectiveness of the existing N&D[*] system, identified its weaknesses, and sought to determine how it can be improved.

The opportunity exists in Nashville for the development of a significant breakthrough in the area of a systems approach to child care services. When the new system becomes fully operational, the present cycle of neglect, anxiety, nutritional deficiency, under-achievement, pre-delinquency, and delinquency can and will be broken for many young people.

Very little data were readily available in the form needed for the study. The team spent six man-months reviewing case folders on 1,200 children to obtain the data base necessary for the study.

To supplement and strengthen the current system, the team proposed particular programs and combinations of programs that are evaluated according to the following objectives:

1.   Reducing the number of N&D petitions filed.

2.   Keeping the N&D child in his home when possible (or at least in a family environment) until the case is disposed of by the Juvenile Court.

3.   Keeping the child in his home or in a family environment when longer-term care is required.

Costs and effectiveness of each proposed alternative program are projected, based largely on an analysis of the current system performance, assuming that the numbers and characteristics of children flowing through the system in 1972 will be the same as they were in 1969. Recommendations for changes are made that would substantially improve the system.

---

[*]N&D is used throughout as an abbreviation for Neglected and Dependent children.

DESCRIPTION OF THE CURRENT SYSTEM

In 1969, 632[1] N&D petitions were filed for such reasons as alleged parental neglect (229 cases), abandonment (60), incarceration (52), emotional difficulties (38), sickness (37), or financial difficulties (31) of parents, and alleged abuse (27).[2]

One-third of the N&D children had been named in one or more previous petitions. One-third of the 13 to 17 year-old N&D children and 45 percent of the 16-year-olds had delinquency records.

Entry of children into the N&D system is through petitions filed at the Juvenile Court Intake Office by parents, police, relatives, neighbors, welfare workers, or even the neglected children themselves in some instances. There were essentially no investigations in 1969-70 to determine if the petitions were warranted. There were no readily available welfare services to keep the children in their homes. There were no attempts to find alternative places for children to stay until the crisis passed.

If children could not stay with their petitioners, they were generally placed at Richland Village (the Metro government's child care institution) until the court hearing two to three weeks later. Three hundred and thirty-two of the 632 N&D children in 1969 were temporarily placed at Richland Village.

In 75 cases where the child had been placed at Richland Village to await court hearing, petitions were withdrawn or informally dismissed prior to court hearing, with the children returning home. In another 20 cases, the court returned the children to their homes or to relatives after the hearings. This raises the question of whether these children should have been subjected to the usually traumatic experience of being removed from their homes, only to be returned at a later date.

The study team found that under the current system, children suffered unnecessarily in the following respects:

A. In 1969, 180 of the 632 children were brought into the system on petitions that were later withdrawn. An effective intake screening process could have kept most of these children out of the system entirely.

---

[1] Excluding about 160 custody petitions filed primarily for administrative purposes.

[2] The remaining 158 were for numerous miscellaneous reasons, each less than 4 percent of the total.

B. Up to 252 N&D children in 1969 could have been kept in their own homes, and 73 in emergency foster homes, if short-term welfare resources had been available.

OPTIONS FOR IMPROVING THE SYSTEM

The team examined four types of programs that are not now being used to improve the short-term performance of the system (between petition filing and court hearing) and two types of programs to improve the longer-term or post-hearing performance.

Intake and Emergency Care

Twenty-Four-Hour-Intake Screening. Round-the-clock screening requires that a welfare worker be on call at all times to investigate each case immediately to determine if there are appropriate grounds for filing a petition. If so, he decides how best to care for the child until court disposition. Such a program could eliminate up to 180 petitions a year and, if resources for short-term care as discussed below were made available, could allow for optimum short-term placement of up to 220 more children. The cost of an in-take screening service would be about $12,000 per year.

Emergency Caretaker Service. An emergency caretaker enters a home and acts as a custodian, but usually stays no longer than overnight. This service is especially effective in cases of temporary abandonment where the parents are delayed in returning home. An emergency caretaker service, at an annual cost of about $5,000, would keep 25-50 children a year in their homes who would otherwise have to be placed at Richland Village.

Emergency Foster Homes. Emergency foster homes are designed to reduce the emotional shock to the children of being taken from their homes by keeping them in a family environment prior to their Juvenile Court hearing. Five emergency foster homes costing a total of $18,000 annually could provide temporary care for about 70 children a year who would otherwise be placed in Richland Village.

Homemaker Service. More than half of the children placed at Richland Village are returned to their homes after a family crisis has abated. Trained homemakers able to give eight-hour or twenty-four-hour service could be used to maintain many of these children in the emotional security of their own homes during the crisis period. Fifteen such homemakers could keep about 150 children a year from being placed at Richland Village, assuming that homemakers were needed twenty-four hours a day; 30 would keep 250 children from being placed there. The annual cost of these homemakers would be $110,000 for 15 or $219,000 for 30.

TABLE I-1

INTAKE AND EMERGENCY CARE —
ALTERNATIVE PROGRAM COMBINATIONS

Program	Current (1969)	Alternatives (Change from Current)			
		I	II	III	IV
24-Hour Screening	No	Yes	Yes	Yes	Yes
Emergency Caretaker	No	Yes	Yes	Yes	Yes
Emergency Foster Homes	2[a]	+5	+13	+5	0
Homemakers	13[b]	+30	+15	+4	0
Children Placed at Richland Village	469	-325	-325	-167	-37

[a]Used for both N&D children and non-N&D children.

[b]Used only for non-N&D children.

INTAKE AND EMERGENCY CARE PROGRAM ALTERNATIVES

Four combinations of the individual programs just discussed are presented as possible choices to supplement the current system (Table 1).

Alternatives:

I. Twenty-four hour intake screening and emergency caretaker service for all children who need them, 30 homemakers serve 91 percent of the children who need them, 5 emergency foster homes serve 85 percent of the children who need them. Three hundred and twenty-five fewer children are placed at Richland Village, compared to 1969.

II. Same as Alternative I, but 8 emergency foster homes are substituted for 15 of the homemakers; the same number of children are served as in Alternative I.

III. Same as Alternative I, but only four homemakers are provided serving only 34 percent of children who need them. One hundred and sixty-seven fewer children are placed at Richland Village, compared to 1969.

IV. Twenty-four hour intake screening and emergency caretaker service only for all children who need them. Thirty-seven fewer children are placed at Richland Village, compared to 1969.

Summary cost and effectiveness estimates for these programs are shown in Table 2 (with further explanations in Chapters IV, V, and VI).

Although Table 2 shows an annual cost after the first year of $179,000 for Alternative I, there are various financing mechanisms that would serve to reduce these costs to the state and metro governments. Under the existing financing arrangements, the state would pay $93,000, metro $51,000 and the federal government the remainder. If Richland Village (which is now a public institution) is converted to a private non-profit institution (thereby making it eligible for funding through AFDC), the annual net cost to the state would be $107,000 and metro would actually save $63,000--the balance would be contributed by the federal government. If Congress approves the Family Assistance Plan as proposed by the Nixon Administration, the annual net cost to the state would be $53,000 and metro would save $106,000 (whether Richland Village is a public or private institution).

LONGER-TERM CARE PROGRAM ALTERNATIVES

A relatively limited analysis of longer-term programs was conducted, but only two options were considered:

24

TABLE I-2

EFFECTIVENESS AND COSTS OF SHORT-TERM ALTERNATIVES

Objectives and Evaluation Criteria[c]	Alternatives							
	I		II		III		IV	
	First[a] Year	Second[b] Year	First[a] Year	Second[b] Year	First[a] Year	Second[b] Year	First[a] Year	Second[b] Year
A.								
1. Reduction in N&D petitions filed[d]	90-200	180-400	Same As Alternative I		Same As Alternative I		90	180
2. Reduction in children in N&D petitions[d]	90-200	180-400					90	180
3. Reduction in families in N&D petitions[d]	36-80	72-160					36	72
4. Cases screened out[d]	90-200	180-400					90	180
B.								
1. Children screened out by 24-hour screening[d]	90-200	180-400	Same As Alternative I		Same As Alternative I		90	180
2. Children avoiding institutional care through use of emergency caretaker	12-25	25-50					12-25	25-50
3. Children avoiding institutional care through use of emergency foster home	36	73	89	179	36	73	0	0
4. Children avoiding institutional care through use of homemaker	126	252	73	146	47	94	0	0
5. Reduction in Children placed at Richland Village	162	325e	162	325e	83	167e	18	37e
COSTS ($000)--Fed., state, and local	106	179	78	124	19	13	12	16

[a] Based on 6 months program development time and only 6 months operating time.
[b] Also applies to the third and following years.
[c] Related to Chapter III.
[d] All five of these evaluation criteria count the same children or families.
[e] This amounts to reductions of more than 12,400 child-days of care (a child-day is one child for one day) for Alternatives I or II, 7,300 for Alternative III, and 300 for Alternative IV (all for the second year only).

1. <u>Intensive casework supervision</u>.   Intensive supervision is ordered when the court feels the family can be maintained as a unit, or when there is no alternative to sending children home. One option considered was to hire one more caseworker at an annual cost of $10,000, thereby cutting the caseload per worker in half. (The study team was not able to assess the effectiveness of current intensive supervision services.)

2. <u>Foster home program</u>.   The Department of Public Welfare sponsors a permanent type foster home program which in September 1970 had 123 homes caring for an average of 380 children. We estimate that 43 to 73 new N&D children per year will require continuing foster care until they become adults. The cost is about $1,300 per child per year.

These programs can be funded under existing Aid to Families with Dependent Children regulations, with the federal government contributing about 45 percent of the costs, the state about 45 percent, and metro the balance. If the proposed Family Assistance Program is implemented, about 81 percent of the costs would be borne by the federal government, 15 percent by the state, and 4 percent by metro.

National Recommendations

This study specifically addressed the problems of N&D children in Nashville-Davidson County, Tennessee. To the extent similar problems are experienced by many other local governments and states, it is possible to offer generalized recommendations that apply beyond Nashville-Davidson. (Recommendations aimed directly at the Nashville-Davidson situation are in Chapter VII.)

1. <u>Establish Central Coordination Among Local Child Care Agencies</u>.

    Child welfare activities tend to be characterized by a lack of coordination. To operate a child welfare system efficiently and effectively, one agency in each city, county or metropolitan area should be given responsibility for coordinated development, research, and planning. The central agencies should function as liaison among federal, state, county, city and private agencies involved in child welfare activities. The major focus should be comprehensive and include long-range planning, follow-through, evaluation and flexibility in the area of program development and promotion. This would relate what the status of the system is at the present time to where the community wants to go in the future.

2. <u>Analyze Child Care Programs as Systems</u>.

    Local governments should undertake evaluations of their neglected and dependent child care programs in terms of their impacts on the children, their families, and the community. These studies should look not only at the individual components but at the system as a whole. This includes the intake process, the juvenile court, children's homes, foster homes, homemakers, adoption activities, case work and so forth. After initial evaluations and setting of objectives, periodic re-evaluations are required to determine how well the system is meeting those objectives. A balanced set of programs should then be developed.

    The term "balanced" as used here, is intended to be more than a vague, general concept. It means that the various components of the neglected-dependent child care system should be provided in a specific mix and at appropriate levels to meet the objectives at an acceptable cost. These should be in conformance with objectives and evaluation criteria such as presented in this analysis (see Chapter III). The study shows that sophisticated mathematical models are not required to conduct such an analysis; but some training in program analysis would be very helpful.

3. Establish and Maintain Linked Records.

      The status and history of children served by a variety of
different agencies, each with their own non-comparable records
systems, cannot be readily determined. This difficulty can be
overcome by establishing (as was done for this study) a linked
records system which includes a composite record on each child,
drawing information from each of the agencies concerned. Such
an information approach permits detailed analysis and identification of corrective actions that would not otherwise show up. Each
major city or county should establish such a system. The main-
tainence of confidentiality is an important requirement of such a
system.

4. Implement Improved Intake and Emergency Care Systems in Other Cities.

      Clearly, significant improvements can be made in existing
systems in most cities and counties throughout the country. Local
governments should examine their intake screening and emergency
care programs in light of the new systems recommended in this
report (Chapter IV).

      Clearly, such improved systems should include as a start
the provision of flexible procedures aimed at avoiding the involvement of the Juvenile Court and the Police Department unless
involuntary removal of custody is required. Priority should be
given to avoiding removing the children from their parents, relatives, or family friends unless there are compelling reasons to
the contrary. In such cases, placement in child-care institutions should be a last resort, used only when other resources
are neither available nor appropriate. This analysis proposes
a balanced set of resources that are both appropriate and not
overly expensive.

      The opportunity exists to achieve significant improvements
in the care of neglected and dependent children; frequently at
very little cost.

5. Provide Subsidies for Adoptions and Increase Efforts to Place Children
for Adoption

      Six states now provide subsidies in appropriate cases for
adopting children in long-term foster care. This is both an appropriate humane and economical practice and should be carried out
by all states. All states should also revise their statutes and
their legal and administrative procedures to make it easier, in
appropriate cases, to terminate parental rights and place children
for adoption.

6. Develop Treatment and Training Programs for Neglected and Dependent Children

    A large proportion of neglected and dependent children are emotionally disturbed or mentally retarded. Effective programs for treating and training such children from lower socio-economic groups do not now exist. An effort should be undertaken at the national level to develop and demonstrate such programs. More specifically, the adaptation of a program like Nashville's successful "Re Ed" (reeducation and training) program to neglected and dependent children should be demonstrated.

7. Conduct a National Demonstration Program of an Emergency Care System

    This study has evaluated an existing system for the care of neglected and dependent children and proposed a more effective new one to replace it. The new system should be tested for at least three to five years in Nashville-Davidson County and carefully evaluated so that its effectiveness can be compared to that of the old system. In order to gain insights as to how typical the Nashville-Davidson situation is, similar demonstrations should be conducted in several other cities. Some planned variations might be incorporated in these different demonstration programs and evaluated to identify the more successful variations.

I. Introduction

This study concerns children who are classified as neglected and
dependent because they suffer from inadequate parental supervision; insufficient food, shelter or clothing, severe physical abuse or neglect by
parents; or dissolution of their family or home. It includes only those
children who are named in Neglect and Dependency petitions filed at the
Davidson County Juvenile Court or who for any reason become residents of
Richland Village. Excluded are children placed voluntarily by parents with
the State Department of Public Welfare, Tennessee Preparatory School, or
voluntary child care institutions. When children go to these state and
voluntary organizations through a Neglect and Dependency petition, however,
they are included. In other words, this report deals only with children
who have officially come into the purview of the Metropolitan Government
of Nashville and Davidson County, Tennessee.[1]

The study deals with child care from the viewpoint of the government
of Metropolitan Nashville-Davidson County. Juvenile delinquency is addressed only to the extent that it relates to problems of Neglected and
Dependent children. Adoptions are addressed only insofar as Neglected and
Dependent children are concerned.

The case files of all children who entered the system between
January 1, 1969 to April 20, 1970 were examined and data coded for computer
processing. However, data gathered at Richland Village covers the period
January 1, 1968 to April 20, 1970. The records of each individual child
from these agencies were linked in the computer file and the data analyzed.
It would have been preferable to collect data over a longer period but this
was not done because there was insufficient time and manpower to collect
much of the pre-1969 data.

Several limitations to this study should be noted:

1. It does not consider causes and prevention of neglect and dependency. Rather, it focuses on child welfare services after neglect occurs.
At this stage, however, the best professional opinion is sought to determine
how such services can be utilized to help prevent recurrences of the problems.

---

[1]How many children who might otherwise be classified as "neglected
and dependent" but have not come to the attention of the Juvenile Court
is not known. If a complainant does not file a Neglect and Dependency
petition, the child is not so classified. The definition of neglect
varies considerably among different persons. Appendix A discusses this issue.

2. Attention is not given to the prospective impact of providing additional income to low income families, such as would be provided by the proposed Family Assistance Plan.[1] Neglect is strongly associated with low income. Perhaps poor persons are more likely to complain of neglect, or their higher population density may convert family problems into community ones. To the extent that added income would change life styles, neglect might be reduced. Additional income also should mitigate against neglect due to inadequate food or clothing.

3. Future need or demand for services is assumed to be essentially the same as the actual demand during 1969-1970.

A latent demand for services might well show up if more services were available. There is no satisfactory way to predict such a contingency, but it could be controlled to some extent by the use of mechanisms such as sliding fee schedules based upon ability to pay.

4. The children studied were followed only for a relatively short period of time. Even though data were obtained on the previous history of each child, this provided a limited perspective of the effectiveness of the child care programs. It would be useful to continue collecting data on these children, preferably until they reach adulthood, as a firmer basis for obtaining a long-term view of program effectiveness.

Most conclusions and statements in this report are based upon data and other information gathered during the study, and from relevant literature. Various gaps in the factual base, however, could not be filled and reliance was placed on "expert opinion" to fill these gaps whenever approximate. In such cases, it is indicated that this was the basis for statements.

Chapter II describes the existing methods of dealing with neglected and dependent children in Nashville-Davidson County. Chapter III defines objectives and evaluation criteria for government programs for these children.

Chapters IV, V and VI analyze various program options for change. Chapters IV and V deal with emergency or short-term care and VI covers longer-term care, wherein the child is removed from his family for an extended period. These chapters describe available options, analyze their effectiveness and costs, consider means of financing, and present an implementation plan.

This study, conducted over an eight-month period concluding at the end of 1970, was a cooperative research project jointly sponsored by the Metropolitan Government of Nashville and Davidson County and the Urban Institute. It required about two man-years of effort, about one-half of it devoted to data gathering and processing. Information available at the beginning of the study was inadequate to identify the major characteristics and effectiveness of the Neglected and Dependent child care system.

---

[1]The financial impact of FAP for child-care programs has been estimated, however, in Chapter V.

There was not enough time or resources to analyze in detail all of the possible alternatives to the current system. Nevertheless, we hope that this in-depth analysis of the system and some of the alternatives we propose will be useful.

Several federal, state, metro and private agencies concerned with services for children and youth participated in this analysis of services for Neglected and Dependent children. They are now actively working together to implement the recommendations in this report. If no changes to the present "non-system" ensue, the effort will have been wasted.

II. Description of the Present System[1]

The flow of neglected and dependent children through the Nashville-Davidson County Juvenile Welfare system is depicted in Figure II-1. The numbers refer to children who entered each point in 1969.

The initiating action is an incident or chronic condition which motivates someone to petition the court to protect the child's welfare.

The number of petitions filed during 1969, categorized by reason, are shown in Table II-1.

Three hundred and forty-eight entrants were under the age of 10; 284 were 10-17 years old. Fifty-two percent of all entrants were male. Seventy-two percent of all entrants were white and twenty-eight percent black.

HOW CHILDREN ENTER THE SYSTEM

Petitions can be filed by parents, relatives, neighbors, the neglected children themselves, police, or welfare workers. Petitions are filed at the Intake Office of the Juvenile Court located at the Juvenile Detention Center. An intake officer is on duty 24 hours a day to accept petitions. He makes essentially no attempt to determine if the petition should be filed. After the petition is filed, the intake officer makes a temporary placement of the child pending Juvenile Court disposition of the case. If the child cannot or should not stay with the petitioner, he will generally be placed temporarily at Richland Village[2] or at a Department of Public Welfare (DPW)[3] emergency foster shelter if he is less than three years old. Figure II-1 shows where the children were temporarily placed prior to the Juvenile Court hearing.

Separate investigations are then conducted by a Juvenile Court probation officer and by a State Department of Public Welfare social worker. On completion of their investigation, which takes about 7-10 days, recommendations are made to the judge. After an average of two to three weeks

[1]Appendix G contains more detailed data.(This is available separately.)

[2]Richland Village is operated by the Metropolitan Social Service Commission.

[3]The Department of Public Welfare is the state welfare agency.

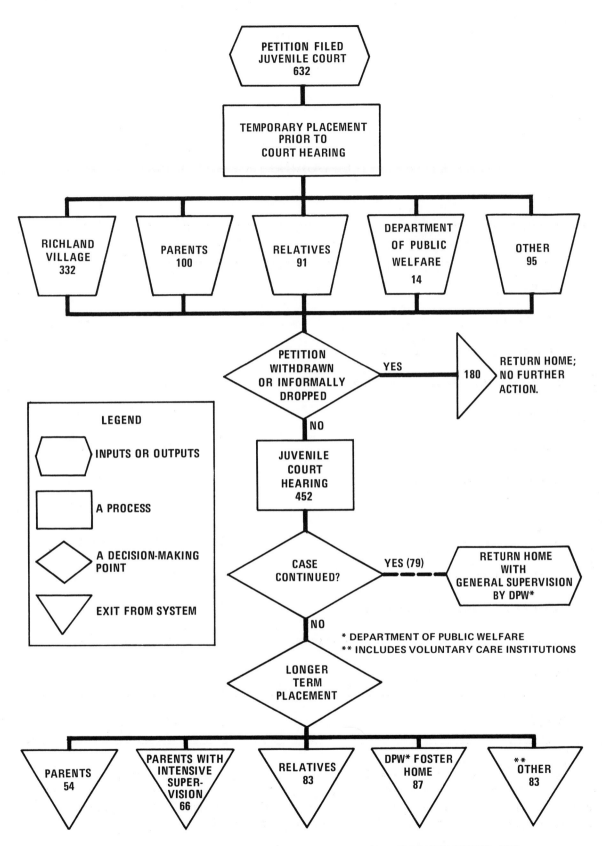

PETITION FILED JUVENILE COURT 632

TEMPORARY PLACEMENT PRIOR TO COURT HEARING

RICHLAND VILLAGE 332

PARENTS 100

RELATIVES 91

DEPARTMENT OF PUBLIC WELFARE 14

OTHER 95

PETITION WITHDRAWN OR INFORMALLY DROPPED — YES → 180 → RETURN HOME; NO FURTHER ACTION.

NO

JUVENILE COURT HEARING 452

CASE CONTINUED? — YES (79) → RETURN HOME WITH GENERAL SUPERVISION BY DPW*

NO

* DEPARTMENT OF PUBLIC WELFARE
** INCLUDES VOLUNTARY CARE INSTITUTIONS

LONGER TERM PLACEMENT

PARENTS 54

PARENTS WITH INTENSIVE SUPER-VISION 66

RELATIVES 83

DPW* FOSTER HOME 87

** OTHER 83

LEGEND

INPUTS OR OUTPUTS

A PROCESS

A DECISION-MAKING POINT

EXIT FROM SYSTEM

FIGURE II-1 FLOW OF CHILDREN THROUGH NEGLECTED AND DEPENDENT SYSTEM, 1969

TABLE II-1

N&D PETITIONS FILED DURING 1969 — BY REASON

Reason	Number	Percent
Neglect	229	36
Abandonment	60	10
Incarceration of parents	52	8
Emotional difficulty of parent(s)	38	6
Sickness of parent(s)	37	6
Request for custody [1]	40	6
Financial difficulty	31	5
Abuse	27	4
Martial difficulty	26	4
Death of parent(s)	22	4
Parent(s) cannot control child	19	3
Inability to find adequate housing	15	2
Other	36	6
TOTAL	632[2]	100

[1]This does not include all of the N&D cases involving request for custody. About 160 cases, where the request was for administrative purposes only and the court was not being asked to protect the physical or emotional well-being of the child, are not counted.

[2]Total number of different children involved was 581; some of the same individuals are in several categories. The total number of different families involved was 274.

following the filing of the petition, the case is heard in the Juvenile Court. However, between intake and hearing, a number of petitions (180 in 1969) are withdrawn by the petitioner or informally dropped.

DISPOSITION OF CHILDREN

Figure II-1 also shows the final disposition of the 632 children named on N&D petitions. Fifty percent (317 out of 632) of all petitioned children were returned home or to relatives without any further supervision by the court or the welfare department. An additional 23 percent (66 intensive supervision cases and 79 continued cases) were returned home under the supervision of the Department of Public Welfare. The remaining 27 percent of the children were placed in Department of Public Welfare foster homes, voluntary organizations (generally institutional settings), or Richland Village (usually pending placement at a foster home or voluntary institution).

Children frequently reenter the system; one out of every three children entering the system has previously had a Neglect and Dependency petition filed. The relationship between neglect and delinquency is illustrated by the extremely high proportion of teenagers on whose behalf Neglect and Dependency petitions are filed who have delinquency records. Table II-2 illustrates delinquency of 1969 N&D children by age bracket.

The Department of Public Welfare foster home program in Davidson County accepts placements by the Davidson County Juvenile Court, and voluntary placements where no court action is taken. In 1969-70, two types of foster homes were operated: two emergency foster homes for placement of under three-year-olds before Juvenile Court action, and 123 permanent homes housing 380 children. In 1969, 87 N&D children were placed in permanent foster homes by the Juvenile Court.

In 1969, 15 N&D children were placed in local or nearby voluntary care institutions and 9 in Tennessee Preparatory School. As of July 1, 1970, only 10 of these 24 children had been discharged. In addition, there were 24 children who had not been declared N&D, but who were referred informally by the Juvenile Court to voluntary care institution.

RICHLAND VILLAGE

Richland Village is a non-delinquent children's home run by the Metropolitan Social Service Commission. About two-thirds of the occupants are neglected and dependent children placed there by the Juvenile Court Intake Office to await court hearing; the remainder are voluntarily placed by the parents, usually through a welfare agency or hospital. Table II-3 shows some of the characteristics of children who were placed in Richland Village.

TABLE II-2

N&D CHILDREN IN 1969 WITH DELINQUENCY RECORDS — BY AGE

AGE	# N&D CHILDREN	# DELINQUENT CHILDREN	% N&D CHILDREN DELINQUENT
10-12	81	9	11%
13	35	7	20%
14	25	10	40%
15	25	8	32%
16	20	9	45%
17	5	1	20%

TABLE II-3

SUMMARY OF CHARACTERISTICS OF CHILDREN AT RICHLAND VILLAGE

Mode of placement

N&D petitions	332
Voluntary	137
Total 1969 placements in Richland Village	469

Age of 1969 entrants (years)

0-9	308
10-17	161

Sex/race characteristics

51 percent male; 49 percent female
70 percent white; 30 percent non-white

Major reason for entry in 1969

Neglect	158
Sickness of parents	75
Abuse	51
Incarceration of parents	42
Emotional difficulty of parents	32
Other	111
Total	469

Destination on discharge - percentages for all children from January 1968-April 1970

Home	51%
DPW foster home	23%
Relatives	7%
Voluntary or state institutions	5%
Other	14%
Total	100%

    Twenty-three percent of the children entering Richland Village between
January 1968 and April 1970 had been there before. Of the children in
Richland Village for the first time, 52 percent stayed more than two weeks
and 30 percent stayed more than one month. Of the repeaters, 80 percent
stayed more than two weeks, 56 percent stayed more than one month, and 23
percent stayed more than 3 months. Other things being equal, it is generally undesirable to keep children away from a family environment for such
long periods.

III. Objectives and Evaluation Criteria

OBJECTIVES

The purpose of this study is to suggest ways to improve the welfare of those children who come to the attention of the Juvenile Court or Richland Village because of neglect and dependency. This requires agreement, first of all, on the objectives to be achieved. Four such objectives are defined:

A. Reduction of the number of N&D petitions filed and the number of children subjected to the system by screening out those cases in which a petition is not justified.

B. Keeping the child in his home when possible (or in a family environment) until a thorough study can be conducted and the disposition of the case is decided.

C. Keeping the child in his home or an appropriate environment when longer-term care is required.

D. Placing the child in a stable environment to which he can adjust, where he will not become neglected again, and where he will not become delinquent.

An auxiliary objective is:

E. Operating the system efficiently so as to minimize the costs of achieving all of the preceding objectives, or to achieve these objectives for the largest number of children when resources are constrained.

EVALUATION CRITERIA

Criteria were devised to measure the extent to which the present system or the proposed supplemental programs contribute to the achievement of the stated objectives. The criteria under "A" and "B" relate to objectives "A" and "B." All of the criteria are used to evaluate the existing program. It is only feasible to project criteria "A" and "B" into the future. The criteria chosen are the following:

A. 1. Number of N&D petitions filed.
    2. Number of different children named on N&D petitions.

3. Number of families which contain one or more children named on N&D petitions.
4. Number of cases screened where a petition was not sworn out.

B. 1. Number of children kept in their own home until Juvenile Court hearing, after which they remain in their home.
2. Number of children avoiding institutionalization because of emergency caretakers.
3. Number of children avoiding institutionalization because of placement in emergency foster homes.
4. Number of children avoiding institutionalization because of homemakers.
5. Number of children placed at Richland Village until a Juvenile Court hearing.

C. 1. Dispositions by the Juvenile Court that are considered to be:

   a. Good.
   b. Questionable.
   c. Bad.

These judgments as to the quality of the disposition are based upon criteria that reflect the following professional opinion:

   a. Families should not be split up and children removed from their parents unless there are compelling reasons to the contrary;
   b. Siblings should be kept together when children are removed from their parents unless there are compelling reasons to the contrary;
   c. A child who needs special attention should not be sent to places where it is not available; for example, a mentally retarded child should not be placed in the care of foster parents who are incapable of handling his problem;
   d. A child should not be returned to his inadequate home because no foster home or other facility is available;
   e. A child under six should not be placed in an institution (including Richland Village) even on a temporary basis, and
   f. A child should not be kept in a temporary care facility more than two weeks on his first stay nor more than four weeks on subsequent stays.

D. 1. The number of children whose adjustment in placement is judged to be: satisfactory; questionable; unsatisfactory.
2. The number of times children are moved from one placement to another.
3. The number of children who are declared N&D more than once.
4. The number of children who have delinquency records.

There are other measures which would be useful for estimating the welfare of N&D children, but which could not be developed within the limited time and resources of this study. These include:

1. Educational achievement. N&D children generally do poorly in school compared to other children.

2. Health status. N&D children generally have poorer health than other children.

3. Long-term adjustment of the child after being declared N&D. This would be reflected by family stability; satisfactory vocational, educational and social progress; and the absence of delinquency and N&D petition. It would be necessary to conduct a long-term study to determine this adjustment with certainty. We have, however, recorded these children's complete records to June 1970 and all their prior delinquency and N&D records.

4. The client's attitude toward the system. It would be useful to interview children and parents who have been subjected to the system to determine their attitudes toward its various components. We were unable to do this because of time and resource limitations, and because the agencies concerned understandably wished to avoid interference with the children, foster parents, etc.

Objectives A and B and their corresponding evaluation criteria apply primarily to the intake and emergency care (short-term) program options analyzed in Chapter IV while C and D apply primarily to the longer-term care options analyzed in Chapter VI.

These criteria reflect broadly the effectiveness of the system as a whole. In addition, each of the programs in the system may have criteria peculiarly appropriate to itself. These "lower level" criteria will be discussed with the individual program options in Chapters IV and VI.

IV. Intake and Emergency Care

This chapter emphasizes an intake, screening, and emergency (short-term)[1] care system aimed at:

--Reducing the number of neglect and dependency cases by screening out those which do not require a court hearing.

--Providing for the immediate welfare of the child by keeping him in his own home when possible until his case can be thoroughly studied, or alternatively, providing for a substitute family environment.

The following four program options for accomplishing these aims are analyzed in this chapter:

1. Revision of Juvenile Court intake screening procedures and related activities.

2. Provision of emergency caretaker service.

3. Provision of additional emergency foster homes.

4. Provision of additional homemaker service.

REVISE JUVENILE COURT INTAKE SCREENING PROCEDURES

The Current Intake System

N&D petitions are sworn out at the intake office of the Juvenile Court which is open 24 hours each day. [2]   There is no attempt to determine

---

[1]Emergency (short-term) care is defined in this report as encompassing the temporary placement and care of the child during the period immediately following an incident (that may result in the filing of a Neglect and Dependency petition) until the child is returned to his parents or relatives or placed for longer-term care in a foster home or institution.

[2]The DPW also maintains an intake service during regular working hours which screens cases involving alleged neglect, abuse, and complaints about inadequate child care. The DPW sometimes requests the Court to declare children N&D (in which case they would be included in this study) and in other cases provides welfare services directly without a petition being

whether or not a petition is justified; when the child cannot or should not remain in his own home there is no search for alternatives to placing the child in Richland Village pending an investigation by the Juvenile Court and the Davidson County office of the Tennessee Department of Public Welfare, and a Juvenile Court hearing (a process that takes about two to three weeks). However, Table IV-1 shows that 60 percent of the children sent to Richland Village by the Juvenile Court in 1969 were later sent home. This raises the question of whether these children should have been subjected to the often traumatic experience of being taken from their homes in the first place, only to be returned at a later date.

In 1969, 332 N&D children were removed from their homes and sent to Richland Village. Discussion here deals with ways to reduce this number of children and to reduce the impact of the N&D process on them. We emphasize that better screening rather than emergency care is needed for those children who do not have to be removed from their homes. Table IV-1 shows the destination of these children after the Juvenile Court hearing. Sending a child to Richland Village causes an emotional impact on the child due to separation from his family, neighborhood and school environment, although it appears to be an attractive, competently operated institution.

The costs of the intake function at the Juvenile Court are not readily separable from costs of other functions. The intake department processes juvenile delinquency cases as well as N&D cases, the latter constituting only about 12 percent of their work·load.[1] After intake has been completed and a temporary placement already made, concurrent investigations are made by the Juvenile Court and the Department of Public Welfare.[2]

In 1969, the Metropolitan Police Department was involved to the extent that, in 35 percent of the N&D cases, they responded to complaints, picked up the children, and signed the petition. Usually they then delivered them to Richland Village and often appeared in court, spending about four man-hours on each case.

---

filed (and would not be included in this study). It handled 602 referrals from July 1969 to June 1970; but it is not known how many of these resulted in N&D petitions being filed. Data relating to these activities are shown in Appendix C. (Available on request.)

[1]632 of 5,357. Juvenile Court of Davidson County, 1969 Annual Report (unpublished).

[2]These investigations are virtually identical. While the Tennessee annotated code requires a DPW investigation, it does not require one by the Court. This inefficient duplication must be weighed against the judge's desire for two investigations.

TABLE IV-1

DESTINATION OF CHILDREN TEMPORARILY PLACED AT
RICHLAND VILLAGE BY JUVENILE COURT IN 1969

Destination	Number	Percent
Return to own home	201	60
DPW foster homes	66	20
Relatives	24	8
Other[a]	41	12
Total	332	100

[a]A few remain at Richland Village until placements elsewhere can be arranged but it is intended to serve only as a short-term care institution.

The Option

The number of N&D petitions can be reduced and the welfare of children can be improved by using a 24-hour intake-screening and placement service with access to emergency caretaker service, homemaker service, and emergency foster home service.

This option requires that a caseworker be on call at all times to immediately work with the family to determine whether there are appropriate grounds for filing a petition.

In 1969, 180 petitions were withdrawn or informally dismissed with no further official Juvenile Court action being taken. Analysis of these cases indicates that a caseworker would have been able to detect most of these cases and prevent petitions being filed.[1] In 75 of these petitions, the child was placed in Richland Village. The analysis uses the conservative assumption that in 50 percent of these cases, placement at Richland Village would have been avoided.

If the petitioner or parents cannot, or should not, care for the child, the investigator must decide whether to:

--arrange for relatives, friends, neighbors, or voluntary community organizations to care for the children;

--send an emergency caretaker into the home to care for the children until the parents return or until the next day;

--place a homemaker in the home to care for the children;

--place the child in an emergency foster home;

--place the child in Richland Village.

The investigator's basic objective, as noted at the outset, would be to keep the child in his own home or a family environment, whenever possible, until a thorough investigation can be conducted, preferably the next day by the same person.

This screening and investigation function would not need a full-time worker, but rather could be the secondary assignment of workers having other responsibilities (or part-time employees could be used). In 1969, the Juvenile Court intake office filed N&D petitions on 218 families[2] who

---

[1]This would have substantially reduced the load on the DPW social workers and Juvenile Court probation officers who must investigate each case for which a petition is filed.

[2]Note the temporary shift of focus from children to families. This is because children are handled as family units when a case is investigated; therefore, "families" is a better indication of work load than "children."

had children placed at Richland Village or emergency foster homes. Based on that experience, the screening and investigation work load would average about 0.6 cases (families) per 24-hour day (with each family having an average of two N&D children).[1] Table IV-2 shows how the 1969 cases were distributed by hour of day and day of week, clarifying why 24-hour screening is necessary. The worker would also relieve the police of a time-consuming job by responding to complaints and picking up the children where neglect or abuse is alleged.

This program might be modeled after the screening service in Los Angeles County, California, which is connected with their "good neighbor homes" (emergency foster home) program. When a law enforcement officer or other source learns of a child who needs help, he contacts the County Department of Public Social Services. During the day, referrals are made to the appropriate district office for the department. After office hours from 5 p.m. to 8 a.m., and on weekends, referrals are routed through a 24-hour telephone answering service to a child welfare worker assigned to be on call in her own home to handle emergency placements. In Los Angeles County, four child welfare workers serve alternately on all-night and weekend duty to provide referral service at all times. The child welfare workers are paid for three hours of overtime when they accept all-night duty and for eight hours of overtime for twenty-four hours of duty on Saturday or Sunday. In Los Angeles County, the Juvenile Court is not involved in the initial screening and temporary placement process.[2]

In Davidson County, the program should be operated by the DPW, but can be operated by the Juvenile Court. Allowing the welfare department to evaluate the case and take one of the actions discussed in this chapter without a petition being filed would obviate the need for so many petitions being filed in questionable cases and allow time for an investigation. Immediate filing of a Neglect and Dependency petition is not legally required as the Tennessee State Code allows removal of children from parents for up to seven days without a petition being filed. The worker would be designated an officer of the Juvenile Court and given the authority to remove children from their homes. The State Code might have to be changed to allow the worker to place an emergency caretaker in the home without parental consent.[3]

---

[1]In 1969, 632 petitions on 581 children from 274 families were filed. However, only 218 of these 274 families had their children removed to Richland Village or an emergency foster shelter pending the Juvenile Court hearing. Had there been an intake screening officer, he would have conducted at least a cursory investigation to determine if the children in these 218 family "cases" should have been removed.

[2]Described in Children, Vol. 16, No. 6, 243. A similar screening procedure is in use in Buffalo, New York.

[3]In the opinion of counsel in New York, where a similar program has operated for several years, if an agency can remove children from a home without the parents' consent, it can also place an emergency parent in the home without their consent.

TABLE IV-2

FAMILIES WITH N&D CHILDREN PLACED BY JUVENILE COURT
INTAKE OFFICE — 1969

Day	Eventually Returned Home or to Relatives	Eventually Placed in Foster Care or With Voluntary Agency	Total
Monday	31	12	43
0-8 a.m.	3	1	4
8 a.m.-4 p.m.	9	2	11
4 p.m.-12 a.m.	4	2	6
Unknown[a]	15	7	22
Tuesday	21	13	34
0-8 a.m.	1	0	1
8 a.m.-4 p.m.	4	4	8
4 p.m.-12 a.m.	6	2	8
Unknown[a]	10	7	17
Wednesday	14	17	31
0-8 a.m.	1	0	1
8 a.m.-4 p.m.	3	6	9
4 p.m.-12 a.m.	3	1	4
Unknown[a]	7	10	17
Thursday	26	11	37
0-8 a.m.	3	0	3
8 a.m.-4 p.m.	5	5	10
4 p.m.-12 a.m.	4	1	5
Unknown[a]	14	5	19
Friday	22	11	33
0-8 a.m.	1	0	1
8 a.m.-4 p.m.	9	3	12
4 p.m.-12 a.m.	4	3	7
Unknown[a]	8	5	13
Saturday	20	6	26
0-8 a.m.	3	3	6
8 a.m.-4 p.m.	7	1	8
4 p.m.-12 a.m.	5	1	6
Unknown[a]	5	1	6
Sunday	11	3	14
0-8 a.m.	1	0	1
8 a.m.-4 p.m.	4	1	5
4 p.m.-12 a.m.	3	0	3
Unknown[a]	3	2	5
TOTAL	145	73	218
0-8 a.m.	13	4	17
8 a.m.-4 p.m.	41	22	63
4 p.m.-12 a.m.	29	10	39
Unknown[a]	62	37	99

[a]Time not recorded in Juvenile Court record.

After the initial disposition as discussed in this section, there will generally be a need for a thorough investigation to determine the child's longer-term welfare. Often there will still be a need for some Juvenile Court action and follow-up action by the DPW or Metropolitan Social Service Commission.

It would take an estimated six months to develop the system. Attention should be given to obtaining the cooperation of various voluntary agencies and groups, including the Council of Community Services, which may be interested in caring for or finding placements for Neglected and Dependent children, pending disposition of their case.[1]

If this intake screening option is implemented, the number of children separated from a family situation and the number of petitions filed would be substantially reduced. Estimates of the requirements for such services are based on the number of children referred for temporary placement by the Juvenile Court intake office during 1969. An important aspect of the effectiveness of this program is the screening out of cases and referral of others to appropriate resources.

Of the 218 family groups of children temporarily placed at Richland Village or in emergency foster homes by the Juvenile Court intake department in 1969, 145 were subsequently returned to their homes or to relatives. The remaining 73 were placed in foster homes or group care facilities. These 145 families should be regarded as particularly susceptible to an emergency parent and homemaker service in their own homes.

More effective screening and investigative capability is related to:

--The ability of caseworkers to judge in which cases the ultimate disposition of the child will be to his home, and in those instances to make decisions which do keep the child in his home.

--The availability of emergency parents, homemakers and emergency foster homes for initial child placement.

--More complete investigative services the following day to determine the type of longer-term care necessary.

Based on examination of the case files, the temporary placements made, and the number of children who ultimately return home or to relatives, the number of N&D petitions filed (632) can be reduced by at least 180 per year without any resources being available other than 24-hour intake screening. A reduction of up to 400 N&D petitions per year is probable if other options discussed later in this chapter are also implemented.

---

[1]Worthy of consideration in connection with screening and placement services is expansion of local day care or baby-sitting services. Some children become N&D cases because parents leave them without sitters. Other N&D children could also receive help from day care facilities. Public and private funds, and cooperative arrangements among mothers, are means for enlarging these services.

Costs

The total costs for this intake screening option properly include the homemaker services, protective services, and community resources required. It is probable, however, that some changes in the distribution of placements could be achieved without expansion of homemaker services and protective services.

The proposed change in procedures would require social workers or probation officers at the Juvenile Court or Department of Public Welfare working at overtime rates plus transportation costs. The total additional costs are depicted in Table IV-3.[1]

There are also significant indirect effects. Under this new screening system, for instance, the police would no longer be involved to the great extent they now are. Under the existing system, the police respond to many complaints of child neglect, actually deliver the child to Richland Village in 33 percent of the cases (including voluntary placements), and actually sign 35 percent of the Neglect and Dependency petitions. If the policeman signs a petition, he must later appear at the Juvenile Court hearing. This function would be better served by the social worker who carries out the proposed screening operation. A minimum annual savings of 830 police man-hours (at a cost of $3,700 in salaries and benefits)[2] would be realized.

The reduction in the number of Neglect and Dependency petitions filed also would result in a reduction in the number of pre-hearing investigations by a Juvenile Court probation officer and Department of Public Welfare social workers. The requirement for immediate screening would roughly counterbalance this saving for one of these agencies; thus, the Department of Public Welfare would still have to conduct the same number of investigations (assuming they operate the 24-hour screening function). The Juvenile Court probation officers could expect a drop of 28 to 63 percent in the Neglect and Dependency cases they currently investigate. As these would be the less severe cases, a commensurate reduction in work load would not be realized; but a 14 to 31 percent reduction (equivalent to .3 to .6 of a probation officer's time at an annual salary cost of $3,700 to $7,400)[2] seems a reasonable estimate of the savings.[3] Roughly equivalent savings in the amount of time the Juvenile Court judge devotes to Neglect and Dependency cases, as well as clerical time savings, would also be realized but cannot be reasonably estimated. None of the savings mentioned in this paragraph are discussed further because it appears likely that the personnel would be reallocated to other functions and no actual dollar savings would accrue.

---

[1]All program costs in this report are based on the 1969-70 actual data. A 10 percent inflation factor was added to reflect anticipated cost increases by 1971-72.

[2]No actual reduction in the cost would occur as the personnel would be reallocated to other functions.

[3]If the duplication between DPW and the Juvenile Court in investigating N&D cases were eliminated, an additional savings in probation officers' time of 1.4 to 1.7 man-years could be realized amounting to about $17,000 to $21,000 in salaries and benefits.

TABLE IV-3
24-HOUR SCREENING COSTS

COSTS	SALARIES	TRANSPOR-TATION	ANSWER-ING SERVICE	TOTAL	INFLATION FACTOR (10%)	TOTAL
Program development (6 months)	4,150[a]	600	-	4,750	475	5,225[d]
Annual operating costs	10,037[b]	970	300[c]	11,307[c]	1,130	12,437[d]

[a]One DPW social worker at an annual median salary of $7,400 plus benefits of $900.

[b]104 weekend days at 8 hours of overtime each; 261 other days at 3 hours each paid at overtime rate (1,615 hours at $3.70 + overtime + benefits).

[c]The answering service can be operated by the present Juvenile Court intake department at no additional costs or by a private answering service for about $300 (based on the Buffalo experience).

[d]The first program year would consist of a program development period for the first six months (at a cost of $5,225) followed by six months of operation (at a cost of about $6,200) - for a total first year cost of about $11,400. The second program year would cost about $12,400.

Intake screening is important in itself. But it is also a key element in each of the other three options proposed. It is assumed, in the following three options, that the first option is an essential first step.

EMERGENCY CARETAKER SERVICES

At the present time, Davidson County has no emergency caretaker service. A number of complaints are received because young children are left without adult or responsible teen-age supervision. There is usually no alternative currently to taking the child to Richland Village. This subjects the children to a traumatic experience when they are removed from their home by strangers, frequently in the middle of the night. In these situations, the parents often appear within a few hours or are located the next day. However, once the children are placed in Richland Village, it takes a court order to get them released, requiring at least several days and usually longer. In 1969 there were 60 children abandoned; 50 of them were abandoned in their own home and could have stayed there with appropriate supervision. Perhaps as few as 25 of them would have needed emergency caretaker service. In the other cases, the case worker would have been able to locate the parents or to find neighbors or relatives to care for the child overnight.

The emergency caretaker would enter the home and act as a custodian until the parents returned or the crisis abated, but would usually stay no longer than overnight. It is necessary for the caretaker to have an emergency kit including blankets, food, cooking equipment, rechargeable flashlight, first aid kit, light bulbs, candy, disposable diapers, insect spray and an aluminum folding cot. The emergency caretaker may be on duty for one week at a time on an on-call basis. A small fee may be paid ($15 per week in Buffalo) for the inconvenience of having to remain near a telephone on call at any time. When the emergency caretaker is called for duty, he is paid an hourly rate, plus mileage. In the event that a person who works days is on duty, there is another emergency caretaker available for daytime emergencies.[1]

In the case of the Buffalo Children's Aid Society, where this program was tested and is now operating as an integral part of their programs, the number of children placed outside of their homes on an emergency basis after having been left alone was reduced from 40 to 50 per year to zero. In 1969, the direct cost was approximately $4,400, including the weekly fee to the emergency parents, small items purchased for the children (food, clothing, etc.), transportation, car, telephone, and incidental expenses.[2]

---

[1]Homemaker service will probably be necessary after the parents return.

[2]Other costs (for the emergency social worker on call and the answering service) were included under the revised screening procedures. See Dorothy Washburn, "Emergency Casework Services, a Review" (Buffalo: Children's Aid Society), October 1970.

As the number of children served in Nashville would be about the same as in Buffalo, the cost (plus an inflation factor) is estimated to be about the same--$4,800. This would provide emergency caretaker service for 25 to 50 children, sparing them from the traumatic experience of being displaced to Richland Village or emergency foster homes. Additional welfare services would be required later for many of the cases.

EMERGENCY FOSTER HOMES

Each year there are some cases in which a child should not or cannot be kept in his home for such reasons as parental abuse, repeated neglect, severe conflicts between parents and child, or occasionally death of a parent. In 1969 there were 73 family cases in which children had to be temporarily placed at Richland Village and were subsequently placed by the Juvenile Court in a foster home or long-term care facility. Of these 73, 42 families with a total of 85 N&D children had one or more children under the age of six. It is particularly undesirable to place children under the age of six in an institution such as Richland Village, according to child care specialists.

Emergency foster homes could be used to house these children, prior to the Court hearing, maintaining them in a family environment and reducing the emotional shock when they are taken from their homes. All of the N&D children in a family, including those over six, would be kept in the emergency foster home to avoid splitting up the family.

Emergency foster homes now are used in Davidson County for children under the age of three. The foster families are paid at a yearly rate, whether a child is kept or not, in order to keep places immediately available. The annual estimated costs of a DPW emergency foster home are depicted in Table IV-4.

An expansion of this program may be accomplished by the DPW or by cooperation with voluntary agencies. The children who would benefit most from emergency foster homes are children under the age of six who have until now been placed at Richland Village, and then later placed in permanent or temporary foster homes or in institutions. As these children should not be separated from their brothers and sisters, the emergency foster homes should accept all the N&D children in the family, even if some are over six years of age. Based on the 1969 experience as to the timing of these cases and their length of stay at Richland Village, Figure IV-1 shows that five emergency foster homes would cover 73 (85%) of the 85 children and nine homes would cover all the children. The cost for five would be about $18,000; the cost for nine would be $32,500.

TABLE IV-4

ANNUAL EMERGENCY FOSTER HOME COSTS

Direct	$1,200[a]
Indirect	362[b]
Total cost per child	$1,562
Average number of children per home	2.1
TOTAL COST PER HOME	$3,280
Inflation factor (10%)	328
TOTAL	$3,608

[a]Payments to foster parents.

[b]Casework, supervision, and other expenses.

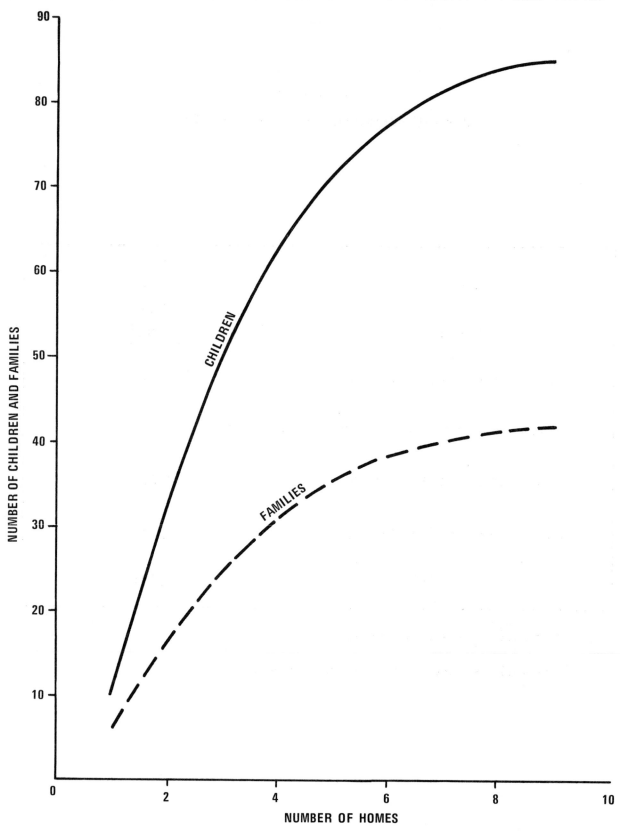

FIGURE IV-1.   EMERGENCY FOSTER HOMES REQUIRED

HOMEMAKER SERVICE

As previously indicated, a large number of children are placed at
Richland Village and then returned home after a stay averaging two to four
weeks. Table IV-5 shows that 203[1] children who were declared N&D for reasons of neglect, parents' illness or incarceration were placed at Richland
Village by Juvenile Court and 125 (62%) of them returned home. In addition,
there were 22 cases involving 65 children (not shown in Table IV-5) who were
voluntarily placed at Richland Village because of sickness of parents; in
most of these cases the children returned to their own homes. With temporary homemaker service, many of these children could be maintained in the
emotional security of their homes instead of being sent to an institution.

Unlike the emergency caretaker service, which must respond at a mo-
ment's notice, go into a home only overnight or for a few hours and be prepared to function without permission of parents, the homemaker service is
a more routine operation. The persons generally go into the home for 8-hour
or 24-hour daily help, are prepared to work a number of days or longer if
necessary, and plan their service to the extent possible with members of
the family.

Homemaker service is presently operated on a limited basis by the
Tennessee Department of Public Welfare in Davidson County. This includes
a trained homemaker who may enter a home, usually when the mother is incapacitated or in some other case in which an adult must be absent from the
home for periods up to eight hours a day. The homemaker is charged with
taking care of the children and the home in the absence of the adult, and
frequently also trains a member of the family in homemaking skills.

Four broad areas of child welfare services in which homemakers, under
the guidance and supervision of caseworkers, could serve effectively in
this option are:

--Providing substitute care for children in their own homes.

--Supplementing and relieving overburdened mothers in the care
  of their children.

--Exploring and evaluating situations in the home.

--Teaching or helping the parent to improve inadequate child
  care and household practices.[2]

---

[1]A preliminary analysis showed that children who entered for reasons of
neglect, illness or incarceration were more likely to be placed in their homes
at Juvenile Court disposition than children who entered for abuse, emotional
difficulty of the parents, etc. Thus, we concentrated our analysis on ways
to keep children in their homes prior to Juvenile Court disposition who were
likely to be returned to their homes rather than on children who ultimately
were likely to be removed from their homes.

[2]Child Welfare League of America, Standards for Homemaker Service for
Children, statement prepared by the Committee on Standards for Homemaking
Service, New York, The League, 1959.

TABLE IV-5

JUVENILE COURT PLACEMENTS IN RICHLAND VILLAGE
BY SELECTED REASON FOR ENTRY AND DISPOSITION — 1969

Reason for Entry	Total	Disposition - Destination on Discharge			
		Home	Relative	DPW[a]	Other[b]
Neglect	147	89	17	31	10
Parent's Illness	14	8	1	5	0
Incarceration of Parent	42	28	2	11	1
TOTAL	203	125	20	47	11

[a]Foster Homes.

[b]Primarily voluntary agencies (largely institutions).

In this option, substitute care for children would be provided when the mother, foster mother, or other person responsible for the everyday care of the children is absent or temporarily incapacitated. A caseworker should evaluate the individual situation before placing the homemaker to determine which of the several methods of child care can best meet the individual needs. The homemaker may be needed for a brief or extended period of time. Homemaker service often provides the most effective way of meeting requests for emergency short-term care. This option may be closely tied to the emergency caretaker option previously discussed, because a homemaker can take over from the caretaker as soon as possible.

Several limitations on the use of homemakers should be cited. There must be a willingness by the parents to accept the homemaker. The homemaker cannot be introduced into situations where the parents are in disagreement. Homemakers may be unwilling to serve for extended periods on a 24-hour basis. Some may not wish to work after dark in certain neighborhoods.

A casework supervisor is required as part of this program to insure that the homemaker services provided are adequate and in the family's best interests.

This homemaker option may also be used for longer-term care following the Juvenile Court disposition of N&D cases.

Thirteen homemakers, each available eight hours per day, (8:30 a.m. to 4:30 p.m.) were being funded by the Department of Public Welfare (DPW) in Davidson County, but they had not been used on many N&D cases.

Table IV-6 shows the total annual cost per homemaker is about $7,300.

A brief period of on-the-job training is sufficient. The DPW homemakers are currently used on an eight-hour per day basis in cases where a mother is ill and someone else in the family is available for the remainder of the day. The number of children who are voluntarily placed at Richland Village due to illness of parents suggests that there are either too few homemakers available on an eight-hour basis or that they are required for up to 24-hour service or on weekends.

Based on the timing and duration of the cases during 1969, plus the voluntary placements at Richland Village due to illness of parents, Figure IV-2 depicts the demand for homemakers as a function of the number of children covered. An additional 22 homemakers could handle all these cases if they were emergency or eight-hour cases. Because of the irregular distribution of the cases, homemakers would work only 13 man-years, however, and substantial slack time would occur unless other uses for homemakers could be found (e.g., for other voluntary cases). Thus we see that only four additional homemakers would be required to cover 94 (34 percent) of the children, fifteen to cover 252 (92 percent), and twenty-two to cover 275 (100 percent). Thus the marginal coverage declines very sharply; particularly after fifteen homemakers.

TABLE IV-6

ANNUAL COST PER HOMEMAKER

Cost Category	Annual Cost
Salaries and Benefits	
Homemaker[a]	$4,700
Supervisor[b]	$1,260
Transportation	$ 700
Sub-Total	$6,660
Inflation Factor (10%)	$ 666
TOTAL	$7,326

[a]One homemaker for one year at $4,200 plus benefits of $500 per year; based on 1970 DPW pay scale.

[b]0.15 of a supervisor at $7,500 plus benefits of $900 per year; based on 1970 DPW pay scale. One supervisor is required per six or seven homemakers.

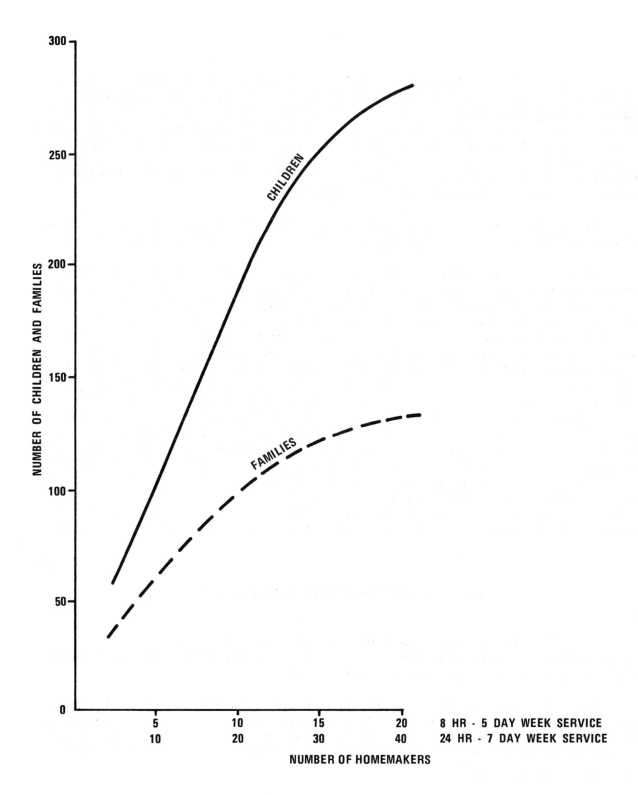

FIGURE IV-2. CHILDREN AND FAMILIES SERVED BY HOMEMAKERS

Figure IV-2 also depicts the number of homemakers required if the same children were served by 24-hour homemakers in lieu of 8-hour homemakers. Twice as many homemakers are required per caseweek on a 24-hour basis compared to an 8-hour basis because a 24-hour homemaker may remain in the home continuously (if necessary) for about 3.5 days and then is relieved by another homemaker. Fifteen homemakers would cover 146 (53 percent) of the children, thirty homemakers would cover 252 (91 percent) of the children, and forty-four would cover all of the children (275).[1]

Table IV-7 shows three different numbers of homemakers using data from the preceding tables and figures, in terms of the children served and cost.

If it does not prove feasible to provide more than fifteen homemakers on a 24-hour basis, either because of a shortage of funds or the inability to hire competent people, emergency foster homes may be substituted. Although emergency foster homes are less effective than 24-hour homemaker service (because the children are removed from their own home), they are still better than placing the children at an institution. Table IV-8 depicts this trade-off, assuming that fifteen 24-hour homemakers were already employed. Thus it considers the options of using either an additional fifteen 24-hour homemakers or eight emergency foster homes.[2] Emergency foster homes are clearly less expensive than 24-hour homemakers, but are less effective. The decision as to which option to pursue depends upon the feasibility of using 24-hour homemakers, the amount of money available, and whether it is believed that the greater effectiveness of 24-hour homemakers is worth the significantly greater cost. Table IV-9 shows a mix of fifteen 24-hour homemakers, and thirteen emergency foster homes; five of the emergency foster homes are for the children who are later to be sent to foster homes or institutions (Figure IV-1) and eight are those shown in Table IV-8.

ALTERNATIVE PROGRAM COMBINATIONS

Thus far the options have been analyzed individually. Now various combinations of these programs are examined in light of the objectives and evaluation criteria discussed in Chapter III.

Four alternative program mixes that would substantially improve the effectiveness of the system and, in fact, create a new system for Neglected and Dependent children are spelled out in Table IV-10. They are in addition to any existing programs. The difference between the mixes is that they

---

[1]The data are based on the practice elsewhere of using a 24-hour homemaker for about 3.5 24-hour days per week and considering this equivalent to an 8-hour, 5-day week. Therefore, one week of 24-hour homemaker service requires two homemakers, while a week of 8-hour homemaker service requires only one homemaker.

[2]Two homemakers are required per family per week on a 24-hour basis while only one emergency foster home is required to serve the same family.

TABLE IV-7

DIFFERENT MIXES OF HOMEMAKERS

Basis	Number of Homemakers	Number of Children Served	Annual Cost[a] ($000)
8-Hour	4	94	29
24-Hour	15	146	110
24-Hour	30	252	219

[a]At $7,300 per homemaker per year (Table IV-6)

TABLE IV-8

TRADE-OFF BETWEEN 24-HOUR HOMEMAKER
AND EMERGENCY FOSTER HOMES[a]

Option	Number of Homemakers or Homes	Number of Children[b] Served	Annual Cost ($000)
24-Hour Homemaker	15	106	110[c]
Emergency Foster Homes	8	106	29[d]

[a]Assumes 15 homemakers are already employed on a 24-hour basis.

[b]Based on the distribution of cases as reflected in Figures IV-3 and IV-4.

[c]$7,300 per homemaker per year (Table IV-6).

[d]$3,600 per home per year (Table IV-4).

63

TABLE IV-9

ALTERNATIVE MIX OF 24-HOUR HOMEMAKERS
AND EMERGENCY FOSTER HOMES

Option	Number of Homemakers or Homes	Children Served	Annual Cost ($000)
24-Hour Homemakers[a]	15	146	110
Emergency Foster Homes	13	179	47
Figure IV-1[b]	(5)	(73)	(18)
Table IV-8[c]	(8)	(106)	(29)
TOTAL	28	325	157

[a]Serves the first 146 children susceptible to homemakers (Table IV-6).

[b]Serves the 73 children particularly susceptible to emergency foster homes (Figure IV-1).

[c]Serves the additional 106 children also susceptible to homemakers (Table IV-8).

TABLE IV-10

COSTS AND CHILDREN SERVED IN FOUR SHORT-TERM PROGRAM COMBINATIONS

Program	First Year[a] No. of Children	First Year[a] Cost ($000)	Second (and each later) Year No. of Children	Second (and each later) Year Cost ($000)
Alternative I				
24-Hour Screening	90-200	11	180-400	12
Emergency Caretaker Service	12-25	2	25-50	5
5 Emergency Foster Homes	36	9	73	18
30 Homemakers[b]	126	110	252	219
Reduction at Richland Village	162[c]	-26	325[d]	-75
TOTAL COST		106		179
Alternative II				
24-Hour Screening	90-200	11	180-400	12
Emergency Caretaker Service	12-25	2	25-50	5
13 Emergency Foster Homes	89	24	179	47
15 Homemakers[e]	73	55	146	110
Reduction at Richland Village	162[c]	-26	325[d]	-75
TOTAL COST		66		99
Alternative III				
24-Hour Screening	90-200	11	180-400	12
Emergency Caretaker Service	12-25	2	25-50	5
5 Emergency Foster Homes	36	9	73	18
4 Homemakers[f]	47	14	94	29
Reduction at Richland Village	83[g]	-17	167[h]	-51
TOTAL COST		19		13
Alternative IV				
24-Hour Screening	90	11	180	12
Emergency Caretaker Service	12-25	2	25-50	5
Reduction at Richland Village	18[i]	-1	37[i]	-1
TOTAL COST		12		16

[a]Based on 6 mos. program development time and only 6 mos. operating time.
[b]24-hour, 7-day per week service.
[c]Amounts to 17 child-years (one child-year is equivalent to 365 days of care for one child).
[d]Amounts to 34 child-years.
[e]24-hour, 7-day per week service.
[f]8-hour, 5-day per week service.
[g]Amounts to 10 child-years.
[h]Amounts to 20 child-years.
[i]Amounts to about one child-year.

include different proportions of homemaker services and emergency foster homes.

Specific program sizes are based on the assumption previously discussed that the same types and number[1] of children will come into the system during each year of the period 1971-1975 as entered during 1969. Undoubtedly, there will be changes, but the nature of these changes and the long-term effectiveness of the programs are uncertain. Therefore, the first two to three years should be considered a demonstration period; the results should be evaluated and the programs and data adjusted accordingly.

All of the alternatives include the 24-hour screening program, and the emergency caretaker program. All of the other program options are dependent upon the 24-hour screening function. And the emergency caretaker program appears so highly effective and very inexpensive that its inclusion is hardly open to serious question.

Alternative I assumes that resources for the programs depicted in Table IV-10 are not severely limited, and the only limitation on program size is the number required to meet the projected demand subject only to "reasonableness." Each of the other alternatives assumes that resources are increasingly constrained and therefore the least cost-effective program options are dropped.

Homemaker service is relatively expensive and subject to the constraint that it will be difficult to get women to work on a 24-hour shift basis and in poor neighborhoods. This program, therefore, bears a major portion of a reduction in resources, decreasing successively in Alternatives II, III, and IV.

Emergency foster homes are not as attractive as homemaker service, but are significantly less expensive. The trade-off here is that being moved to a different home causes more emotional disturbance among children-- particularly younger children--than would be experienced if they remained in their own home with a homemaker (and possibly together with one or both parents). But homemakers are less appropriate in cases of abuse, when parents are quarreling, etc. There is no precise technique for calculating this trade-off. In Alternative II, eight emergency foster homes are sub- stituted for fifteen 24-hour homemakers at an annual reduction in cost of $80,000.

Table IV-11 shows the effectiveness and costs of the short-term alter- natives in light of criteria discussed in Chapter III. Obviously, Alter- natives III and IV would serve comparatively large numbers of children at lower costs compared to Alternatives I and II. This is because the latter two alternatives include large quantities of 24-hour homemaker service and emergency foster homes for the more difficult cases; productivity for these two programs is lower due to the uneven distribution of the cases.

---

[1]Six hundred thirty-two children.

TABLE IV-11

EFFECTIVENESS AND COSTS OF SHORT-TERM ALTERNATIVES

Objectives and Evaluation Criteria[c]	Alternatives							
	I		II		III		IV	
	First[a] Year	Second[b] Year	First[a] Year	Second[b] Year	First[a] Year	Second[b] Year	First[a] Year	Second[b] Year
A.								
1. Reduction in N&D petitions filed[d]	90-200	180-400	Same As Alternative I		Same As Alternative I		90	180
2. Reduction in children in N&D petitions[d]	90-200	180-400					90	180
3. Reduction in families in N&D petitions[d]	36-80	72-160					36	72
4. Cases screened out[d]	90-200	180-400					90	180
B.								
1. Children screened out by 24-hour screening[d]	90-200	180-400	Same As Alternative I		Same As Alternative I		90	180
2. Children avoiding institutional care through use of emergency caretaker	12-25	25-50					12-25	25-50
3. Children avoiding institutional care through use of emergency foster home	36	73	89	179	36	73	0	0
4. Children avoiding institutional care through use of homemaker	126	252	73	146	47	94	0	0
5. Reduction in Children placed at Richland Village	162	325[e]	162	325[e]	83	167[e]	18	37[e]
COSTS ($000)--Fed., state, and local	106	179	78	124	19	13	12	16

[a] Based on 6 months program development time and only 6 months operating time.

[b] Also applies to the third and following years.

[c] Related to Chapter III.

[d] All five of these evaluation criteria count the same children or families.

[e] This amounts to reductions of more than 12,400 child-days of care (a child-day is one child for one day) for Alternatives I or II, 7,300 for Alternative III, and 300 for Alternative IV (all for the second year only).

The higher cost of Alternative I compared to II is due to the more extensive use of 24-hour homemaker service. In Alternative II, eight additional emergency foster homes are used to replace the last fifteen of the thirty homemakers in Alternative I. This trade-off was shown to take account of possible decreased funds and uncertainty as to whether homemakers could be used so extensively; emergency foster homes are the next most effective option. As it is preferable to keep the children in their own homes whenever possible, homemakers are preferred over emergency foster homes. The decision is whether to use Alternative I, which gives better service, or Alternative II which is cheaper. Alternative III dominates Alternative IV because, by the second year, it is both more effective and less costly.

V. Financing Intake and Emergency Care

Currently, the programs affecting Neglected and Dependent children in Nashville-Davidson County are financed by a complex mix of federal, state, and Metro funds. Richland Village and the Davidson County Juvenile Court (insofar as it pertains to Neglected and Dependent children) are financed entirely by Metro funds. Sixty percent of the Neglected and Dependent children who entered Department of Public Welfare foster homes during the study period were financed under AFDC (Aid for Dependent Children).[1] Under this program, the federal government pays 75 percent of the cost; the Tennessee Annotated Code specifies that the state pay 20 percent, and Metro 5 percent. The remaining 40 percent of the children (ineligible for AFDC) are financed by either state or Metro funds. The Metro government contributed a total of $95,000 for this purpose during fiscal year 1970-71.[2]

AFDC funds could pay for the costs of the alternatives presented in this report to the extent that eligible children are served. If it is assumed that the 60 percent of AFDC eligibles in the foster home program would be typical of all the programs in question, the cost impact on the alternatives may be estimated.

The Law Enforcement Assistance Administration (LEAA) currently provides funds for 60 percent of approved programs (with up to 75 percent in certain special cases) with the state and local government providing the remaining 40 percent. Due to the relationship between neglect and delinquency and the current emphasis in the LEAA upon prevention and rehabilitation, it is possible that the options in this study could qualify for funding.

Other possible funding sources include research and demonstration funds of various federal agencies, notably the Office of Economic Opportunity and the Department of Health, Education and Welfare.

The proposed federal Family Assistance Plan (FAP) includes a new Title XX to the U.S. Social Security Act that would considerably expand federal funds for child welfare services. Of particular interest to this study is the provision for payments of $300 for each child in foster care (including both private and public institutions such as Richland Village) plus 75 percent of all other costs for child welfare services. The Nixon

---

[1]Administered by the U.S. Social Security Administration.

[2]This includes funds for both N&D children and voluntary placements.

administration withdrew this proposed amendment in 1970 but promised to resubmit it in the first session of the 92nd Congress.[1]

Table V-1 depicts the federal, state and local shares of the program costs shown in Table IV-10 under the three financing alternatives: AFDC, LEAA, and FAP. AFDC should be considered the most likely funding source, as it is available at present. LEAA is also potentially a funding source, but it is not very likely that its funds will be allocated to these programs. FAP is the most attractive potential funding source since it offers the largest federal contribution, but it has yet to be enacted.

In addition, some children in Richland Village are potentially eligible for AFDC, although the State Welfare Commission currently does not include them under the program. This is due to a provision in Section 204 of the U.S. Social Security Act that specifies that children in public institutions are ineligible for AFDC, but children in private non-profit institutions are potentially eligible. As it is unlikely that this provision will be changed (unless Congress approved the proposed Family Assistance Plan), consideration should be given to changing Richland Village from a public to a private non-profit institution.

Table V-2 shows the projected costs of Richland Village, less the savings from Table IV-10, under two alternative assumptions:

(1)   Richland Village remains a public institution and

(2)   Richland Village becomes a private non-profit institution.

Substantial savings of $68,000 to $110,000 annually would be realized by the Metro government under the second assumption.

Table V-3 shows the projected costs of Richland Village, less the savings from Table IV-10, under two other alternative funding mechanisms:

(1)   LEAA

(2)   FAP.

Clearly, substantially larger savings would accrue to the Metro government, particularly if FAP were implemented.

Table V-4 shows the combined effects of Tables IV-10 through IV-14.

----

[1] U.S. Senate, HR 16311 The Family Assistance Act of 1970. June Revision. Revised and submitted to the Committee on Finance of the Administration, November 5, 1970.

TABLE V-1

FINANCING ALTERNATIVES — SHORT TERM

	First Year [e]			Second (and each later) Year		
	AFDC[b]	LEAA[c]	FAP[d]	AFDC[b]	LEAA[c]	FAP[d]
Short-term						
Alternative I						
Total[a]	106	106	106	179	179	179
Federal	48	64	80	81	107	134
State	55	42	21	93	72	36
Local	3	--	5	5	--	9
Alternative II						
Total[a]	66	66	66	99	99	99
Federal	30	40	50	45	60	74
State	34	26	13	51	39	20
Local	2	--	3	3	--	5
Alternative III						
Total[a]	19	19	19	13	13	13
Federal	9	11	14	6	8	10
State	9	8	4	7	5	3
Local	1	--	1	--	--	--
Alternative IV						
Total[a]	12	12	12	16	16	16
Federal	5	7	9	7	10	12
State	7	5	2	8	6	3
Local	--	--	1	1	--	1

[a]From Table IV-1.

[b]75 percent federal, 20 percent state, 5 percent local for eligibles (60 percent).

[c]60 percent federal, 40 percent state (assuming the state runs the programs).

[d]75 percent of total.

[e]Based on 6 mo. program development time and only 6 mo. operating time.

TABLE V-2

RICHLAND VILLAGE FINANCING — PUBLIC VS. PRIVATE INSTITUTION

	First Year [d]			Second Year		
	Public	Private [c] (AFDC)	Differ- ence	Public	Private [c] (AFDC)	Differ- ence
Alternative I or II						
Total[a]	97	97	--	194	194	--
Less Savings[b]	26	26	--	75	75	--
Net	71	71	--	119	119	--
Federal	--	32	+32	--	54	+54
State	--	9	+ 9	--	14	+14
Local	71	30	-41	119	51	-68
Alternative III						
Total[a]	97	97	--	194	194	--
Less savings[b]	17	17	--	51	51	--
Net	80	80	--	143	143	--
Federal	--	36	+36	--	64	+64
State	--	10	+10	--	17	+17
Local	80	34	-46	143	62	-81
Alternative IV						
Total[a]	97	97	--	194	194	--
Less savings[b]	1	1	--	1	1	--
Net	96	96	--	193	193	--
Federal	--	43	+43	--	87	+87
State	--	12	+12	--	23	+23
Local	96	41	-55	193	83	-110

[a]Total Richland Village costs shown in Appendix E inflated by 10%.

[b]Richland Village savings from Table IV-10.

[c]Richland Village becomes a private, nonprofit institution and qualifies 60 percent of its children for AFDC (the same percentage as in the DPW foster home program). The federal government, under existing regulations, pays 75 percent, the state 20 percent and Metro 5 percent of the costs for eligible children, plus all the costs for the ineligible children.

[d] Based on 6 mo. program development time and only 6 mo. operating time.

TABLE V-3

RICHLAND VILLAGE FINANCING — FAP AND LEAA

	First Year [e]		Second Year	
	LEAA[c]	FAP[d]	LEAA[c]	FAP[d]
Alternative I or II				
Total[a]	97	97	194	194
Less Savings[b]	26	26	75	75
Net	71	71	119	119
Federal	43	58	71	98
State	--	10	--	17
Local	28	3	48	4
Alternative III				
Total[a]	97	97	194	194
Less savings[b]	17	17	51	51
Net	80	80	143	143
Federal	48	70	86	128
State	--	8	--	12
Local	32	2	57	3
Alternative IV				
Total[a]	97	97	194	194
Less savings[b]	1	1	1	1
Net	96	96	193	193
Federal	58	87	116	175
State	--	7	--	14
Local	38	2	77	4

[a]Total Richland Village costs shown in Appendix E inflated by 10 percent.

[b]Richland Village savings from Table IV-10.

[c]The federal government would pay 60 percent and the Metro government 40 percent under existing regulations.

[d]Based on the proposed Title XX of the Family Assistance Plan (FAP) the federal costs are derived by the formula on the following page:

[e]Based on 6 mo. program development time and only 6 mo. operating time.

TABLE V-3 (footnote d continued)

Define:

    A = Number of children at Richland Village in 1969.
    B = Reduction in number of children at Richland Village.
    C = Net number of children at Richland Village.
 300C = FAP fixed contribution of $300 per child.
    D = Net costs at Richland Village (this table).
 TFC = Total federal contribution.

Then:

    (1) $C = A - B$
    (2) $TFC = D - (300C)\ .75 + 300C.$

It is assumed that the state would pay 80 percent and Metro 20 percent of the costs not covered by the federal government as is now done for AFDC eligibles.

TABLE V-4

NET STATE AND LOCAL COSTS
(Change from the Base)

	First Year[f]				Second Year[e]			
	AFDC[a]	AFDC[b]	LEAA	FAP	AFDC[a]	AFDC[b]	LEAA	FAP
Alternative I								
Net State Costs	55	64	12	31	93	107	72	53
New Programs[c]	(55)	(55)	(12)	(21)	(93)	(93)	(72)	(36)
Richland Village[d]	--	(9)	--	(10)	--	(14)	--	(17)
Net Metro Costs	3	-38	-43	-63	5	-63	-71	-106
New Programs[c]	(3)	(3)	--	(5)	(5)	(5)	--	(9)
Richland Village[d]	--	(-41)	(-43)	(-68)	--	(-68)	(-71)	(-115)
Alternative II								
Net State Costs	34	43	26	23	51	65	39	37
New Programs[c]	(34)	(34)	(26)	(13)	(51)	(51)	(39)	(20)
Richland Village[d]	--	(9)	--	(10)	--	(14)	--	(17)
Net Metro Costs	2	-39	-43	-65	3	-65	-71	-110
New Programs[c]	(2)	(2)	--	(3)	(3)	(3)	--	(5)
Richland Village[d]	--	(-41)	(-43)	(-68)	--	(-68)	(-71)	(-115)
Alternative III								
Net State Costs	9	19	8	12	7	24	5	15
New Programs[c]	(9)	(9)	(8)	(4)	(7)	(7)	(5)	(3)
Richland Village[d]	--	(10)	--	(8)	--	(17)	--	(12)
Net Metro Costs	1	-45	-48	-77	--	-81	-86	-140
New Programs[c]	(1)	(1)	--	(1)	--	--	--	--
Richland Village[d]	--	(-46)	(-48)	(-78)	--	(-81)	(-86)	(-140)
Alternative IV								
Net State Costs	7	19	5	9	8	31	6	17
New Programs[c]	(7)	(7)	(5)	(2)	(8)	(8)	(6)	(3)
Richland Village[d]	--	(12)	--	(7)	--	(23)	--	(14)
Net Metro Costs	--	-55	-58	-93	1	-109	-116	-188
New Programs[c]	--	--	--	(1)	(1)	(1)	--	(1)
Richland Village[d]	--	(-55)	(-58)	(-94)	--	(-110)	(-116)	(-189)

[a]Richland Village remains a public institution and does not qualify under AFDC: but new programs qualify.

[b]Richland Village becomes a private non-profit institution and qualifies under AFDC; new programs also qualify.

[c]From Table V-1.

[d]From Tables V-2 and V-3.

[e]Also applies to each later year.

[f]Based on 6 mo. program development time and 6 mo. operating time.

VI. Longer-Term Care

The two previous chapters focus on choices for possible improvement
in emergency or short-term child care, while the cases of N&D children
are pending a hearing by the Davidson County Juvenile Court.

At the hearing, the judge decides who should have custody of the child
over the longer term. This chapter deals with the longer-term program,
with special emphasis on those children who cannot be returned to their
families without some supervision, or who must be removed and placed outside the home.

The objectives in longer-term care are those discussed earlier in
Chapter III, to keep the child in his home or an appropriate alternative
and to place him in a stable environment where he will adjust well, where
he will not again become neglected, and where he will not become delinquent.

The process for determining the child's placement for longer-term care
may be reviewed briefly. While the child is still in emergency placement,
concurrent investigations are conducted by a Juvenile Court probation officer
and DPW social worker. Each submits a separate report to the judge in time
for his hearing, normally scheduled two to three weeks after the N&D petition is filed. The judge then decides where to place the child.

The disposition of children in 1969, based on these decisions, is
shown in Figure II-1. Of the 632 children on whose behalf N&D petitions
were filed, 317 (50 percent) were returned home or to relatives without any
further supervision by the court or by the welfare department. (Of these,
180 petitions were withdrawn or informally dismissed, 54 of the children
were returned to parents, and 83 were placed with relatives.)

Seventy-nine children (12 percent) were returned home with some general
supervision by the Department of Public Welfare; an additional 66 (10 percent) were returned home under "intensive supervision" by the Department of
Public Welfare, and the remaining 170 (27 percent) were placed in the custody
of DPW foster homes, voluntary organizations that generally placed the children in institutional settings, or Richland Village (usually pending placement from there to foster homes or voluntary institutions).

POSSIBLE OPTIONS FOR IMPROVEMENT

It must be stated emphatically at the outset that the data for assess-
ing present practices and especially for projecting the impact of changes

in the longer-term aspects of N&D care are extremely sketchy, not only in Nashville-Davidson County, but also throughout the country. Even answers to basic questions about the value of case work and the response of children to various long-term situations have not been determined with any assurance. The tentative statements as to the effectiveness of the alternatives presented in this chapter, therefore, reflect the present uncertainty that pervades this field.

With that caution, the following options are considered:

--Lowering the case loads of those carrying out intensive supervision.

--Increasing the number of temporary and permanent foster homes.

--Creating assembled families' homes.

--Subsidizing adoptions.

--Using Richland Village as a residential treatment center.

LOWERING THE CASE LOADS OF THOSE CARRYING OUT INTENSIVE SUPERVISION

Intensive supervision by the DPW is ordered by the Juvenile Court judge when he feels a child should be kept in the family unit or when there is no alternative to sending the child home. In either case, the family appears unable to meet the child's needs without professional assistance, so intensive supervision is ordered until the family is able to function in an acceptable way by itself.

The present load of intensive supervision caseworkers is 29 cases. This is a relatively light load compared to other types of welfare services, but many social workers feel that the difficulties of this kind of supervision and the value of more personal attention to both the child and parents may produce improved results.

The program's effectiveness is not measured here in terms of the quality of the child's adjustment during the long-term care, although this would be desirable if the necessary data were available. Instead, attention is placed on "petitions later filed"--in other words, on the filing of new Neglect and Dependency petitions on the same children, indicating particularly severe breakdowns of the rehabilitation or adjustment efforts.

Table VI-1 depicts the effectiveness of the current intensive supervision program in avoiding new N&D petitions for children who entered this program during three recent time periods. Of the 37 children placed in the program from January 1 to June 30, 1969, there were 17 (46 percent)

TABLE VI-1

INTENSIVE SUPERVISION CASES
JANUARY 1, 1969 — JUNE 30, 1970

Status as of July 1, 1970	Period When Child Was Placed in Intensive Supervision		
	January 1 to June 30, 1969	July 1 to December 31, 1969	January 1 to June 30, 1970
With family (no petition filed)	20	19	20
Petition later filed	17	10	0
TOTAL	37	29	20

for whom N&D petitions were filed by July 1, 1970. For the two later periods, less time had elapsed in which petitions could be filed.[1]

Cases under intensive supervision are "high risk" to begin with. So it is to be expected, as Table VI-2 shows, that a significantly higher percentage of them had repeat N&D petitions than did children sent to parents or relatives without Department of Public Welfare supervision. Caseworkers questioned about the apparently high 46 percent rate of repeaters stated that the performance for supervised families is "not bad" considering the serious problems encountered. Without hard proof to substantiate it, some social workers further suggest that reducing caseloads from 29 to 15 cases per worker would lead to a reduction in repeat cases.

It should be clarified that major expansion of the intensive supervision program itself is not warranted in terms of the children covered. Of the children sent to families without supervision in 1969, a review by social workers turned up only 12 cases[2] in only four families whose placements might have suggested some supervision. So the option of decreasing the case load is a question of more intensive care for the same cases now in the program. This option may be viewed in three ways:

Reduce the case loads from 29 to 15 per worker. In 1969, each case included an average of about two children, had an average duration of one year, and the equivalent of one caseworker was required to handle this work. Reducing the load by 50 percent would require one additional caseworker. Without broaching the difficult matter of measuring the competency of the caseworkers, and assuming that there might be a benefit from giving greater attention to each case, the additional costs are estimated as follows:

Salary and benefits for one caseworker	$8,300
Transportation	400
Additional cost	8,700
Inflation factor of 10 percent	870
TOTAL ADDITIONAL COST OF THIS OPTION[3]	$9,570

Reduce the caseload by screening out those who are least likely to succeed. Evaluation tools for predicting success are imprecise.[4] But more

---

[1]There was no significant difference in the percentage of new N&D petitions by age groups (0 to 5, 6 to 12, and 13 to 16 years).

[2]This constituted 22 percent of the children sent to families without supervision.

[3]No increase in overhead or indirect cost is assumed as the number of cases remains the same.

[4]A diagnostic team could attempt this.

TABLE VI-2

CHILDREN PLACED WITH PARENT(S) OR RELATIVES
JANUARY 1 – JUNE 30, 1969

Status July 1, 1970	Intensive supervision		No supervision	
	Number	Percent	Number	Percent
No additional petition filed	20	54	33	72
Petition later filed[a]	17	46	13	28
TOTAL CASES	37	100	46	100

[a]The difference in "petition later filed" between "intensive supervision" and "no supervision" is significant at the .05 level (df = 1, X^2 = 5.81).

careful screening would mean that the number of children placed in foster homes or voluntary care institutions (or possibly sent home without supervision) would be increased. It would be very difficult to estimate how many cases might be changed from one category to another by this kind of diagnostic effort.

Eliminate the intensive supervision altogether. This would mean sending all the present intensive supervision cases to foster homes or voluntary care institutions (or possibly sent home without supervision). This would save approximately $9,600 now spent for casework, plus possibly some of the health care or other special services often provided. Foster care for these 60 children at about $1,300 per child would cost up to $78,000 a year for an indefinite period. Voluntary institutions would cost even more, although private groups might bear a portion of the burden. These cost factors leave out the subsequent impact on the welfare of the children. Clearly about half of the children now successfully responding to intensive supervision would be unnecessarily removed from their parents.

EXPANDING TEMPORARY AND PERMANENT FOSTER HOMES

Another option for improving longer-term care for N&D children is to increase the number of temporary and permanent foster homes available. This might involve (1) more of the current type of homes that are operated predominantly by lower-income families, (2) more middle- and upper-income foster families, and (3) higher pay to increase the number and quality of available homes.

The Department of Public Welfare foster home program accepts both N&D cases and voluntary placements arranged without court action. The emergency homes serve children under three years of age and others awaiting Juvenile Court action, while permanent homes accept primarily children for whom no other early disposition appears likely.

The program grew rapidly from July 1969 to September 1970 with a 46 percent increase in foster homes and a 41 percent increase (including court and noncourt cases) in numbers of children. This growth, seen in Table VI-3, stemmed from the availability of more Aid to Families with Dependent Children funds (Title IV-A, Social Security Act), the backlog in the number of children requiring foster family care, and from successful recruitment of foster parents.

Looking at the N&D cases alone, Table VI-4 shows 104 foster children from January 1969 through June 1970.

The performance of the foster home program may be measured by three priorities:

--The highest priority is returning the children to parents, relatives or guardians. This occurred for only 14 children.

TABLE VI-3

DPW FOSTER HOMES — FOR BOTH N&D AND VOLUNTARY CASES
JULY 1, 1969 TO SEPTEMBER 30, 1970

	July 1969	Sept. 1970	Percentage Change
Foster homes	84[a]	123[b]	46
Children in foster homes	270	380	41

[a]An additional 16 homes were not in use and were later closed. These were deemed to be substandard.

[b]An additional 30 applications from prospective foster parents had been screened and were being considered.

TABLE VI-4

DEPARTMENT OF PUBLIC WELFARE FOSTER HOME PROGRAM — N&D CASES ONLY

| Status-July 1, 1970 | Entered Foster Home | | | | | | | |
| | January to June 1969 | | July to Dec. 1969 | | January to June 1970 | | Total | |
	Number	Percent	Number	Percent	Number	Percent	Number	Percent
In same foster home	10	46	30	85	39	83	79	76
Sent to another foster home	4	18	0	0	4	9	8	8
Returned to parent(s), relative or guardian	8	36	3	9	3	6	14	13
Unknown	0	0	2	6	1	2	3	3
TOTAL	22	100	35	100	47	100	104	100

--The second priority is to have children who cannot be taken back into their own homes adopted. This happened for <u>none</u> of the children in the program. (More about adoptions will be discussed as a separate option later in this chapter).

--The third best choice, if the child remains in the foster home, is to achieve stability and satisfactory adjustment. The 76 percent who stayed in the same foster home during the period studied implies a high degree of permanence and stability. Adjustment, as judged by a psychiatric social worker, was found to be "reasonably good" in 66 percent of the cases and "probably bad" in only 8 percent.[1] See Table VI-5. (These ratings, based on observations over a short span, should be rechecked at least after several years and preferably after the children become adults, since the best measure of childhood adjustment is their later degree of productivity and participation as members of the adult society).

The growth in foster homes, already referred to, was accomplished without any increase in payments to the foster parents. The payments, set by the DPW, have several components. The <u>initial</u> (one-time) payment on entry of a child into a foster home ranges from $40 to $100, varying with the special needs of the particular child. The <u>monthly</u> payment ranges from $64.50 to $84, depending on age.[2] Table VI-6 shows the costs of the entire foster home program (N&D plus voluntary placements) for fiscal year 1969-70. The $1,335 cost per child includes $852 of direct service costs to the foster parents for room, board and other expenses.

These costs do not necessarily reflect an <u>equitable</u> payment to foster parents for care of a child. National studies, not conducted in Nashville, show that foster parents generally contribute additional funds from their own pockets. At best, the foster home payments are at the lower range of what it costs the typical family to support a child.[3]

---

[1] These ratings were determined on the basis of the child's psycho-social functioning reflected in the case file. In unclear cases, the child's caseworker and the foster care supervisor were consulted and a rating determined. Thirteen cases (10 percent) were coded "unknown" as insufficient information was available to determine the quality of adjustment.

[2] Monthly payments $30 to $35 higher are authorized under certain circumstances such as when children require special care or are placed in a child-care institution.

[3] Based on Department of Labor "Cost Estimates for Urban Family Budgets," the added annual cost to a typical Nashville family of providing for another child ranges from $747 to $1,344. The lower figure reflects the additional cost experienced by a husband and wife under 35 years of age living at an "intermediate level," for a second child under six years. Their total family income is $5,376. The higher figure is the additional cost experienced by a husband and wife 35-54 years of age for a second child (the first is 6-15 years). Their total family income is $7,466. The cost at a "higher level"

TABLE VI-5

DEPARTMENT OF PUBLIC WELFARE
FOSTER HOME PROGRAM

QUALITY OF ADJUSTMENT IN FOSTER CARE (Children Placed 1 January 1969-30 June 1970 Status as of 1 July 1970)		
Quality of Adjustment	Number	Percent
Reasonably Good	69	66
Questionable	14	13
Probably Bad	8	8
Unknown[1]	13	13
TOTAL	104	100

[1]Insufficient information available to determine quality of adjustment.

TABLE VI-6

FOSTER HOME COSTS (Fiscal Year 1969-70)[a]

Costs	Actual $
Direct Service	$281,330[b]
Administrative	119,436[c]
Total	400,766
Children in Care	
Children Served	456[d]
Average During Year (Child-Years)	330[d]
Cost Per Child-Year	1,214[c]
Inflation Factor (10%)	121
TOTAL	$ 1,335

[a]Ending June 30, 1970.

[b]Predominantly payments to foster parents.

[c]Predominantly costs of case workers and supervisors.

[d]456 individual children were served; but the average number during the year was 330.

[e]This average cost is about the same as the cost of serving additional children (marginal cost).

86

TABLE VI-7

CHILD/MONTHS OF FOSTER CARE AND COSTS FOR A FIVE-YEAR PERMANENT FOSTER HOME PROGRAM
PROGRAM YEAR

Year During Which Children Placed	1		2		3		4		5		Total	
	Child/ Mos. (00's)	$000	Child/ Mos. (00's)	$000	Child/ Mos. (00's)	$000	Child/ Mos. (00's)	$000	Child/ Mos. (00's)	$000	Child/ Mos. (00's)	$000
1	3-4[a]	29-48[b]	5-9[c]	57-97[d]	5-9	57-97	5-9	57-97	5-9	57-97	23-40	257-436
2			3-4	29-48	5-9	57-97	5-9	57-97	5-9	57-97	18-31	200-339
3					3-4	29-48	5-9	57-97	5-9	57-97	13-22	143-242
4							3-4	29-48	5-9	57-97	8-13	86-145
5									3-4	29-48	3-4	29-48
TOTAL	3-4	29-48[b]	8-13	86-145	13-22	143-242	18-31	200-339	23-40	257-436	65-110	715-1,210

[a]Derived by equalizing the placements of the 43 and 73 children for each month of the year.

[b]Child-months (257 or 437) x cost per child-month ($111).

[c]Assumes the same number of children continue for the second year (43 and 73 x 12).

[d]Child-months (516 or 876) x cost per child month ($111).

The DPW is now concentrating recruitment efforts on middle- and upper-class families, and the results from persuasion or public education should be assessed before changes in payments are offered. But then it would be useful to find out whether higher pay would attract more and higher quality foster parents. Then, if it is known that a certain additional number of foster homes are needed, it could be ascertained (assuming increased payments are found to increase the supply) how much monetary inducement would be required to achieve that goal.[1] Payments adequate to meet the actual costs incurred by the foster parents should be an important consideration.

The children for whom the additional permanent foster homes are needed would come from several sources. One category includes those currently sent home without supervision but where the quality of placement was deemed "bad" or "questionable" (12 children in 1969. A petition was later filed on one of these.) A larger category includes children sent home with intensive supervision but whose situations are considered unsatisfactory (previously discussed). It may be noted that the N&D children sent to foster homes in 1969 numbered 57, but as more homes became available, the annual rate during the first half of 1970 rose to 95.

The increased rate is probably partially due to the increased number of foster homes available. This suggests a demand for approximately 57 to 95 new foster home placements. If the number of children sent home or to relatives from foster homes remained about the same (about 23 percent, implied by Table VI-4), and the intake and turnover rates were reasonably constant, 43 to 73 new foster homes would be required to handle placements for Neglected and Dependent children.[2] Table VI-7 shows that the cost for the first year would be about $29,000 to $48,000 for 257 to 437 child-months of care (at $111 per child-month). For each succeeding year, these same children would be served for an entire year amounting to 516 to 876 child-months; but additional children would also become Neglected and Dependent and require foster home placement. Thus each row in Table VI-7 shows the child-months of foster care and the costs for children placed initially during each of five years. Clearly, placement of children in

---

is $1,858 at a total family income of $10,325. See Bureau of Labor Statistics Bulletin 1570-2, "Revised Equivalence Scale," December 21, 1970, Washington, D.C., for estimating details.

[1]For example, if the payment level were raised from about $70 per month to about $100 per month, how many more foster parents could be found and how would the quality of care change; or conversely, if an additional one hundred foster parents are required, what change in the inducement would be necessary to obtain that number.

[2]This assumes, consistent with the findings of Maas and Engler, that after a year in foster care, there is little chance that the child will ever return home or be adopted. The turnover rate is therefore assumed to be zero after the first year in foster care; Henry S. Maas and Richard E. Engler, Jr., Children in Need of Parents (New York: Columbia University Press), 1959. Because very few children over the age of 12 are placed in foster homes, it is assumed that none of the children placed during the five-year period become adults and leave foster care.

permanent foster homes implies an increasing commitment of resources each year. This is because relatively few children return home or to relatives and none are adopted. Thus, these children must remain in foster care until they become adults while, at the same time, additional children are placed in foster care each year.

These projections of entry and attrition rates in foster homes must be used with caution. The past experience on which the estimates are based could be changed somewhat or even drastically by various elements of the child care system--such as the use of homemakers, more intensive supervision, and the availability of foster homes themselves--or by external matters such as liberalization of welfare regulations, the state of the economy and so forth. Subject to wide variations in precise numbers, however, the need for substantially more foster homes is clearly indicated at this time.

CREATING ASSEMBLED FAMILIES' HOMES

A related option envisages the establishment of assembled families' homes, each of which could take care of about five children. Such homes have been extensively used in Washington, D.C.[1] They are found appropriate for cases involving large numbers of children in the same family when it is not desirable to split them up, when there is little likelihood of returning them to their parents, and when there is little hope of their being adopted. They are useful for emotionally disturbed or mentally retarded children, whose handicaps require specially trained foster parents and access to special services.

The Washington assembled families' program attempts to stabilize conditions for children expected to remain in foster care indefinitely, until adulthood. Unique features distinguishing assembled families from conventional permanent-type foster family homes include the following:

--The foster mother is a salaried employee of the agency.

--The agency rents the home or pays a rental supplement.

--Payments for children are based on actual living expenses rather than prescribed formulas.

--Limited relief help--essentially "babysitting" service--is provided.

--Larger numbers of children are served than in most foster family homes (five compared to an average of two or three).

The program has succeeded in offering stable environments and in promoting adjustment. After an average 32 months of care, 90 percent of the children

---

[1] Family and Child Services of Washington, D.C., The Development of Group Foster Homes for Children in Long-Term Care, June 1968.

were still in the same home, and 88 percent of the children were rated as experiencing "adequate" or "better than adequate" adjustment. The average total cost in 1970 was $4,020 per child/year.[1]

The costs and effectiveness of the D.C. project may not fairly be compared with the current DPW foster home program because (1) The assembled family homes accept only permanent care cases while the DPW accepts short-term cases as well; (2) the average length of stay was 32 months in the assembled families' homes, at the time data were collected, while the average length of stay of children placed in DPW foster homes in 1969 was less than one year (as of July 1, 1970), so, more time had elapsed in which turmoil could occur in the homes; and (3) the "quality of adjustment" determinations in the two situations were based on subjective judgments of different caseworkers using different scales of measurement.

While this option attracted interest as a means of stabilizing the environment of children who must remain in foster care, the cost is too great to merit further attention to it by Nashville-Davidson at this time.

SUBSIDIZING ADOPTIONS

Adoption is widely agreed to be preferable to indefinite stays in foster care or private institutions. There are several major constraints to increasing the number of adoptions:

--Parents may be unwilling to surrender the child, and involuntary court termination of parental rights has not been successfully pursued, despite the fact that Tennessee has a liberal adoption statute permitting involuntary termination of parental rights in appropriate cases.

--It often is difficult to find parents to adopt children who are black, handicapped, older, etc. In some cities, intensive publicity campaigns have helped overcome this.

--Adoption is often too costly to those who would consider it. Currently, foster care payments cease when a child is adopted. Some cities have found it possible to increase the number of adoptions by providing continuing financial support for a specified time period. This is particularly attractive when the alternative may be for the child to remain in foster care until reaching adulthood. The benefits to the child from adoption are very significant. Even from a cost standpoint, such an alternative is attractive, as payments are no more than the cost of maintaining the child in foster care, and may be reduced gradually in successive years.

---

[1]This is a reasonable approximation of the cost per _additional_ child (marginal cost) as fixed costs were a very small proportion of total costs.

The concept of subsidy after adoption is being promoted actively. Laws allowing public agencies to give financial support to families that adopt children have been passed in seven states--Maryland, New York, California, North Dakota, Michigan, Illinois and Minnesota. Prospective parents and children are now denied the opportunity for adoption due to financial constraints. This is especially true if the child is black, mentally or physically handicapped, etc.

In New York, the only one of these states from which data are available, it has been estimated that each subsidized adoption will save the state $8,550 by the time the child reaches adulthood.[1] There were 302 subsidized adoptions from September 1, 1968, when the law took effect, to June 30, 1970; these constituted only 4 percent of total adoptions in the state.

This option clearly merits consideration for humane as well as economic reasons.

USING RICHLAND VILLAGE AS A RESIDENTIAL TREATMENT CENTER

If some of the choices set forth in this study are accepted, one important result will be a significant decline in the child population of Richland Village. The adoption of Alternatives I or II in Chapter IV would cause a reduction of 325 placements per year, reducing the average population by about 60 percent.[2] This conforms with the general de-emphasis on placing children in institutions among child care professionals.

This does not mean that the facility may not be used to promote improvements in the care of N&D children. This option is to convert or partially convert Richland Village into a residential treatment center for neglected and dependent children.

The model for such a treatment center might be the unique re-education or "Re-Ed" program developed in Nashville at Cumberland House. This is a training program for emotionally disturbed children. The Re-Ed program so far has been applied only to middle-class children whose families are willing to cooperate.[3] It remains to be seen, of course, whether the N&D children from a lower socio-economic strata will respond as well, particularly

---

[1]This figure was derived by comparing the amount of the subsidy with what it would have cost had the child remained in foster care.

[2]The reduction in placements would be from 469 in 1969 to 144 under alternatives I or II; the average population would decline from 57 to 25.

[3]Bower, Eli M. et. al., "Project Re-Ed, New Concepts for Helping Emotionally Disturbed Children" (Nashville, 1969).

if their parents are unwilling or unable to participate.[1] Also, the Re-Ed
program has not dealt with mentally retarded children.

This option is tentative and requires testing for the above reasons.
But the large proportion of N&D children who are emotionally disturbed or
mentally retarded strongly suggests the need for dealing directly with
these handicaps. Treatment and rehabilitation go far beyond the discussions up to this point about merely providing adequate care.

The Re-Ed program is one of the rare instances of successful treatment
of emotionally disturbed children. A two-year follow-up of children treated
at Cumberland House concluded that 90 percent had adjusted satisfactorily.
The costs averaged about $35 to $40 per child-day. The average stay was
about six months per child, for an average cost of about $7,200.

Translating these costs to the N&D program, there would be the incre-
mental costs of care at Richland Village plus the specific costs associated
with the Re-Ed project itself. The total costs have not been developed.

Two possible alternative programs for Richland Village were specified
in the recent "Five-Year Comprehensive Plan for the Improvement of Law
Enforcement in Metropolitan Nashville-Davidson County, Tennessee."[2] These
were both given top priority in the plan for juvenile justice. The first
called for using Richland Village as a residential treatment and rehabilitation program for juvenile delinquents. The second called for using the
facility for training youths (they may be neglected and dependent) who have
academic and behavioral problems. Each program was estimated to cost
$210,000 (see copies of proposals in Appendix F).

PROGRAM LEVELS FOR LONGER-TERM CARE

Based on the analyses presented earlier, Table VI-8 depicts the anticipated program levels for the next five years for more intensive supervision and for expansion of foster home programs. (Due to insufficient
data, similar projections cannot be made with confidence for the other
attractive options--subsidized adoptions, or new uses of Richland Village.
It should be noted that these could have an impact on the foster home programs, depending on their magnitude and effectiveness, but no such estimate
of this impact is attempted here.)

It will be recalled that a constant load of 60 children is projected
for the intensive supervision program, with the possible change to two case
workers instead of one. In the case of foster homes, however, the assumption
(see Table VI-7) is that the annual net placements will continue to increase
by 43 to 73 children per year, and that they will remain in foster homes

[1]But the Department of Public Welfare can require the parents to cooperate as a condition of the parents keeping the children.

[2]The Administration of Justice Planning Agency, "Thou Shalt Not Ration
Justice," (November 1970).

TABLE VI-8

PROGRAM LEVELS — LONGER-TERM

Program	Unit Title	Program Year 1[a] Units	$000	2 Units	$000	3 Units	$000	4 Units	$000	5 Units	$000	Total Cost Units	$000
Intensive Supervision	Children Served (actual)	30[b]	5	30[b]	10	30	10	30	10	30	10		45
Permanent & Temporary Foster Homes[c]	Child-Months (hundred)	3-4[d]	29-48	8-13[e]	86-145	13[f]-22	143-242	18[g]-31	200-339	23[h]-40	257-436	65-110	715-1,210
TOTAL		-	34-53	-	96-155	-	153-252	-	210-349	-	267-446	-	760-1,255

a6-months only.
bThe total of 60 children served per-year does not change under this option. This is the number of children served by the additional case worker (for which the costs are shown) for six months during the first year and 12 months for each later year. The existing case worker will handle the other 30 children for a total of 60.
cFrom Table V-7.
d43-73 children.
e86-146 children.
f129-219 children.
g172-292 children.
h215-365 children.

TABLE VI-9

FINANCING ALTERNATIVES – LONGER TERM

Source of Funds	YEAR 1			YEAR 2			YEAR 3			YEAR 4			YEAR 5		
	AFDC[b]	LEAA[c]	FAP[d]	AFDC	LEAA	FAP	AFDC	LEAA	FAP	AFDC	LEAA	FAP	AFDC	LEAA	FAP
Total[a]	43	43	43	125	125	125	202	202	202	280	280	280	356	356	356
Federal	19	26	29	56	75	95	91	121	165	126	168	227	160	214	289
State	19	17	13	55	50	24	89	81	30	123	112	42	157	142	54
Local	5	-	1	14	-	6	22	-	7	31	-	11	39	-	13

[a] From Table V-8, taking the mid-point of the ranges of total cost cited there.

[b] Seventy-five percent federal, twenty percent state, and five percent local for eligible children (sixty percent of total children).

[c] Sixty percent federal, forty percent state (assumes the state provides all the matching funds).

[d] Three hundred dollars per child plus seventy-five percent of remaining costs.

until adulthood. Since few foster children are over 12 years old, practically none of them will reach adulthood in the five-year period that is projected.

FINANCING THE TWO PROJECTED OPTIONS

Three approaches to paying for the programs just discussed (assuming an average of the ranges quoted in Table VI-8) are developed in Table V-9, showing the variations in federal, state and local shares of the financing burden.

The three mechanisms for financing, AFDC, LEAA, and the proposed FAP, are discussed in Chapter V and need not be detailed again here. FAP, of course, has not yet been enacted, so its inclusion is understood to indicate "if and when Congress acts." The LEAA funds theoretically are available for these programs; yet because these funds are limited and many high priority crime-related programs compete for them, LEAA participation in terms of LEAA's present budget and policies must be described as not probable. This would leave the AFDC alternative which requires more state and metro funds. If LEAA funds became available, the cost to Metro would be less than under the other two mechanisms.

VII. Recommendations

A new system incorporating the following components, should be implemented immediately:

Implement One of the Proposed Short-Term Alternatives

One of the four alternatives already outlined for intake screening and emergency care should be implemented. The choice will depend on available funds, success in mobilizing community participation, and cooperation among interested agencies.

Provide Subsidies for Adoptions and Increase Efforts to Place Children for Adoption

No N&D children were adopted during the period in question. The State of Tennessee should follow the lead of other states and provide subsidies for adopting these children. The Department of Public Welfare should increase its efforts to terminate parental rights and place N&D children for adoption.

Expand the Department of Public Welfare Foster Home Program and Intensify Supervision

The expanded foster home program and the more intensive DPW supervision suggested in Chapter VI should be implemented.

Expand the Role of Richland Village

If one of the short-term alternatives is implemented, Richland Village will have substantial unused capacity and the remaining residents will be primarily children who are either emotionally disturbed or older. Serious consideration should be given to partially converting it to a residential treatment center. Tennessee's own Re Ed program, in Nashville, now trains and educates emotionally disturbed children who are not neglected and dependent. Its adaption to N&D children should be explored.

Make Richland Village Eligible for Federal Subsidies

Unless federal regulations are changed so that children residing in public facilities can become eligible for payments under the Aid to Families with Dependent Children (AFDC) program, Richland Village should be converted to a private non-profit institution in order to qualify for this federal assistance.

Develop a Continuing Data Collection and Evaluation Effort

To determine how well the N&D system is meeting its objectives, a continuing information-evaluation effort is needed. A prototype data collection and management information system, developed as part of this study, is now in use on the Metro government's computer. It can be readily used to gather data on a routine basis, and should be strengthened to include additional information about specific characteristics of the children. After the system has operated for one to three years, the data should be carefully evaluated and the new system compared to the old to determine efficiency and effectiveness. A longer-range study should also be conducted which would follow the children into adulthood.

Establish Central Coordination

There is no central coordination of the present "non-system." In order for the proposed new system to operate efficiently, an agency should be created or identified as having responsibility for coordinated program development, research and planning. This agency should function as liaison between all public and private agency activities involved in effective utilization of community resources. The major focus should be comprehensive, and include long-range planning, follow-through, and flexibility in the area of program development and promotion. This would relate where we are now to where we want to go during the next decade.

Train Team of Professionals and Generalists

The provision of community services for children is characterized by a mixture of professional specialists, each particularly competent in some very specific aspect of child welfare. The system needs generalists in addition to specialists. These generalists will have to be trained to understand and manage the total system. This team approach requires lateral entry into the system from the outside; a process which is not now possible due to civil service restrictions. These restrictions should be relaxed. Provisions must also be made for training programs geared toward broad and flexible professional competencies. These competencies might incorporate skills in education, psychology, social work, public administration, and systems management.

Promote Citizen Involvement and Provide for Child Advocacy

To defend the well being of children who are in the care of local governments according to standards satisfactory to Nashville-Davidson parents in general, a substantial number of citizens should be trained and involved in the child welfare programs. These citizens can act in volunteer capacities that acquaint them with goals and practices of the N&D system. Child advocacy should be carried out to further the objectives of the child welfare programs.

Promote Cooperation Between Universities and Government Agencies

The Nashville Urban Observatory, set up to help promote cooperation between local universities and government agencies, should mobilize available expertise to develop imaginative new child care programs, as well as to support existing ones.

Three-to Five-Year Program Recommended

The components above outline a comprehensive system of services for pre-delinquent children in the Metropolitan Nashville community. The development, installation, implementation, and evaluation will require three to five years.

Appendix

APPENDIX A

Estimating the Universe of Need of Neglected and Dependent Children for Available Services

A recent publication of the Child Welfare League of America stated, "The concept of 'need' is widely used in social work, but the task of defining the concept so that it can be utilized in research is difficult and complex."[1]

In contrast to the difficulties in measuring need, it is relatively easy to determine demand based on an analysis of the request for specific services during a specified period of time. Although many studies of demand have been made, these consist of intake studies carried out by individual agencies and therefore address primarily the services provided by that particular agency. A few intake studies have been conducted by welfare councils or other planning bodies that analyze placement demands for total communities.

The Child Welfare League of America (CWLA) recently approached the problem of measuring the demand or need for foster care. They concluded that a

> significant study of "true need" in relation to child placement is not possible. First, we lack the means for accurate measure of parental functioning that would be needed to identify family situations where children can be considered to require placement. Second, the complex and multi-faceted nature of the problem indi-·cates the unfeasibility of conducting interviews of sufficient depth and breadth on a voluntary basis with a sufficiently large representative sample of the families on so sensitive a subject.

The CWLA studies use a middle-range concept of demand, with recognition that this is an underestimation of "true need." CWLA concluded that demand is closer to true need in child placement than in almost any other welfare program, since the problems precipitating placement are usually the result of crucial or urgent needs, are highly visible, and represent an issue of great concern to the general community.[2] In support of their view, CWLA noted that reviews of intake patterns of several agencies indicated that the bulk of requests came from community sources rather than the families

---

[1] Child Welfare League of America, "The Need for Foster Care," 1969. See also Genevieve W. Carter, "Measurement of Need" in Norman Polansky (ed., Social Work Research, Chicago: University of Chicago Press, 1960), p. 201-223.

[2] Child Welfare League of America, "The Need for Foster Care," 1969.

themselves. Consequently, the families' motivation for service seemed less likely to affect the volume of service requested in child placement than would be true in other areas of services.[1]

In a study of seven cities, however, an attempt was made to obtain information on all requests for foster care received by agencies in the cities. During a three-month period (April through June, 1966)

> ...it was assumed that requests for foster care (i.e., expressed need) would provide some approximation of the actual need for such care. Our findings with respect to differences among the cities and the volume of requests, and the problems precipitated in their requests, and in the types of placements requested, bring this assumption into question. They indicate that requests for services are strongly influenced by the services that are available. What is reported here, therefore, is expressed need which may approximate true need in some communities but not others.[2]

Three-fourths of the children covered in this survey were white. In every community the portion of nonwhite children in the sample was much higher than the proportion of nonwhites in the general population; but in communities with a relatively small nonwhite population, the difference was much greater than elsewhere. The authors concluded that it is reasonable to assume that under-representation of nonwhites reflects, in part at least, the lesser availability of service.[3]

Our report is consistent with the first view, in that we use experienced demand as an indication of need. It must be recognized that if the demand for service is very sensitive to the supply (availability), then our estimate of demand may be understated.

Nationally, the number of children in foster care (including foster family homes and institutions) is expected to increase from 287,200 in 1965 to 364,000 in 1975, for an annual increase of about 2 percent. This estimate uses the series B census projection of the 1975 population, but the 1970 census suggests that the series D projection is more accurate. The series D projection would result in 322,200 in 1975, or an annual increase of slightly more than one percent.[4]

---

[1]Ibid., pages 2-3.

[2]Ibid., p. 70.

[3]Ibid.

[4]Based on U.S. Department of Health, Education, and Welfare,"Foster Care of Children, Major National Trends and Prospects," 1968. Assumes the rate of children in foster care increases from 4.0 per 1,000 children under 18 years of age in 1965 to 4.7 in 1975 (which is a linear extrapolation of past trends).

Other factors may influence the projected number of Neglected and Dependent children. While the number of N&D children increased during 1968-1969, the trend during 1970 was distinctly downward, although we gathered data for only about the first four months of the year. One can hypothesize that the very large increase in the Davidson County AFDC and Foster Home caseloads are at least partially responsible.[1] Also, the poverty population (the group that produces the majority of neglected and dependent children) is decreasing. Conversely, many child welfare professionals believe that the number will probably increase, and that there could be a latent demand for the services.

We can offer no precise method of accounting for these factors. We will assume that there will be no change from the 1969 situation during the next five years.

---

[1]Between July 1969 and September 1970, the AFDC caseload increased from 2,818 to 4,357--an increase of 55 percent and foster homes from 84 to 123, or 46 percent.

APPENDIX B

Findings of the Joint Commission
on Mental Health of Children

The Joint Commission on Mental Health of Children offers several conclusions and recommendations resulting from their evaluation of the social services aspects of child welfare that are relevant to this study.[1] Generally, the Commission concluded that services for children and youth are grossly inadequate, antiquated, and poorly coordinated, and that there is a dramatic mismatch between the character of the services offered for children in need and the needs and rights of the children. They concluded that even if financial investments in the present system were multiplied several times over, massive inefficiencies and suffering would continue because the system is in need of drastic restructuring.

The Commission found the following "pervasive, inherent inadequacies in many aspects of the service system":

1. Systems tend to be oriented to keeping the professions constant and stable rather than to meeting the needs of the children being served.

2. The systems are oriented toward remedial crises services, rather than preventive programs designed to alleviate the causes preceding an underlying crisis. Different agencies tend to respond separately to a series of discrete crises which arise in the life of the child. There is often no communication between different agencies which handle the same child.

3. The systems are ill-coordinated and serve only a small fraction of the population in need and at risk. Poor coordination occurs within and between agencies--between those that give similar service and those which should not compete with each other.

4. The systems tend to serve those clients most likely to achieve success on the agencies' terms rather than those most in need.

5. Overlap is noted in the systems.

6. The system tends to be highly traditional and conservative, even in the programs it labels as innovative.

---

[1]Report of the Joint Commission on Mental Health of Children, New York: Harper and Row, 1969.

In addition to these deficiencies, the Commission also identified a series of "second order" problems "relating to management and policy making at agency, neighborhood, city, state and national levels." These problems are the following:

1. Unsystematic methods of data collection which result in an oversupply of fragmentary, confused data and an almost total absence of usable operating and management data directed toward problem solution.

2. Pressing problems in the system which are defined differently at every level and rarely are these differences examined so that meaningful priorities can be established.

3. No agency takes responsibility for a central overview of services affecting the well-being of children at any level. Even at the national level, little attention is given to policy questions of long-term importance.

4. Research tends to be disconnected from operating practice.

The Commission recommended the creation of various advocacy bodies to serve as agents to sort out functions and to eliminate the present confusion, fragmentation and overlap between and among agencies and systems of services. The Commission also recommended the establishment of a President's Advisory Council on Children which would undertake, among others, the following activities:

1. Identify the actual and presumed goals toward which agencies, programs, or groupings of these, operate.

2. Explore the experience gained in successful arrangements in the United States and those in other countries which represent approaches to total service systems for children.

3. Explore alternative strategies for obtaining service goals with particular attention to those not restricted by the boundaries of traditional practices and programs; (e.g., payments to mothers for raising children as an alternative to public assistance).

4. Formulate and lay the groundwork for experiments in delivering high quality child center services based on our best current knowledge.

5. Formulate systems of data gathering and identify analogies with successful service systems which will lead to formulation of models of management information systems which can be implemented, in prototype fashion, at city and state levels.

The Commission particularly stressed the need for coordination of social welfare services and policies in all levels of government, and the need for coordination between public programs and voluntary agencies in order to prevent duplication and ill-coordination of services and to insure the availability of programs and services.

In the area of adoption and foster care (including institutional care) the Commission stated that "within the present non-system children often land in foster care without adequate evaluation of their needs. The present reliance on social, legal and clinical labels for placement is inadequate." Specifically, the Commission recommended financial and other assistance to the "underdeveloped parts of the child welfare system." These included (a) expansion of adoptive services; (b) homemaker, day care, and extended day and baby sitter programs; (c) full range foster care programs; (d) group care programs; and (e) community based institutional care. A child development council was recommended to provide leadership in the development of more effective formal working arrangements between agencies (including schools, courts, mental health centers, and child welfare agencies, etc.). This child welfare council would be sensitive to the views and needs of consumers and parents. Particularly stressed was the need to protect children in the context of substitute care. It particularly mentioned the maintenance of existing friendship patterns through mechanisms such as payment of relatives for taking care of children just as foster parents are paid.

The Commission recommended research to acquire information regarding foster care, including how much is needed and for what types of children; and determination of the consequences of various foster care decisions. To meet this need, it recommended:

1. Research should be conducted, based on a national sample census of families undertaken, in order to arrive at a meaningful estimate of the number who need supportive, supplementary and substitutive services.

2. Several service and research centers should be established in various regions of the country with the objective of innovation and research follow-up; they should determine the consequences of alternative courses of action, and serve as demonstration and training centers.

3. Grants should be made specifically to encourage feedback research in foster care agencies.

It also found that a child's emotional disturbance is frequently related to the family situation (interpersonal relations, marital problems, etc.). The cause and effect relationship is not clear, however, because of the intricate behavioral situations in the functioning of the family members and their relationships with the larger social system. It is therefore extremely difficult to arrive at a clear understanding of the various causative factors in the emotional and mental disorders (p. 417).

Although parent education programs seem to be an interesting possibility, evidence in the form of existing programs suggests that such programs have not had a measurable impact on parental attitudes and behavior. (pp. 539-40). Nevertheless, the Commission still felt that parental education should be used.

The Commission called for:

(1) A better diagnosis of the causes of children's problems;

(2) homemakers (8- and 24-hour service);

(3) payments to relatives for keeping children;

(4) group care especially for pre-adolescents and adolescents;

(5) day care centers for housing projects; and

(6) adoption if the parents are incompetent (p. 536).

APPENDIX D

Data System

Approximately 50,000 items of data on nearly 1,200 children were collected in developing the data base for this study. It was essential to gather this much data to be able to characterize the children currently flowing through the system, measure the flows of children through various elements of the system, evaluate the performance of the current system, and to estimate the anticipated performance of the proposed options.

Sources of Data

The primary sources of data were:

1. Juvenile Court files for all N&D children from January 1969 to April 1970.

2. Richland Village files for all children in residence between January 1, 1968 and April 20, 1970.

3. Tennessee Department of Public Welfare, Davidson County Office. Case files for all children identified above who were placed in DPW foster homes.

4. Board of Education files for all N&D children in the Metro School System who were administered Stanford-Binet or WISC intelligence tests.

Collection of Data

The data were collected by two-man teams who searched through the case folders on each of the children considered. Each team was led by a social worker or by an advanced graduate student in psychology. Almost all of the data could be extracted without requiring interpretation. The only entries requiring professional opinion and interpretation were for "quality of (Juvenile Court) disposition" -- (Juvenile Court recording sheet, col. 45) and for "quality of adjustment in foster home" -- (Department of Public Welfare recording sheet, col. 53).

It was a tedious, painstaking job to locate all of the case folders and to understand and code accordingly what had happened to the child in the many complex cases uncovered. Approximately six man-months were expended on the effort. Data could be gathered easily for a continuing or on-going evaluation by providing appropriate forms to be filled in at such times as intake, court hearing, and departure from the system.

The data were coded and recorded on IBM FORTRAN 80 column coding forms for keypunching and eventual computer-assisted analysis. Partial coding instruction keys for Juvenile Court, Department of Public Welfare, and the Board of Education data are shown in Tables D-1, 2 and 3, respectively. In retrospect, it would have been useful to have gathered family socio-economic data and child intelligence and handicap data from the Juvenile Court files. The probation officers frequently included these data in their case investigations. A copy of an actual Juvenile Court DPW combined coding sheet with the last names blanked out to preserve confidentiality is reproduced in Figure D-1.

Quality control checks were conducted to determine how accurately the data were coded. This was accomplished by randomly selecting samples of coded cases and comparing the data coded with the case file from which the data were originally drawn. The error rates were not high enough to change any of the findings.

The Richland Village data showed a random error rate of 1.6 percent; none of the errors were systematic. The check on the Juvenile Court data showed a random error rate of 0.5 percent and one systematic error in coding. As we were not able to correct for this error, we did not use that element of data. The check of the Department of Public Welfare data showed a random error rate of 1.3 percent. No checks were made on the Board of Education data.

Data Reduction and Analysis

Data reduction, cross-tabulation, specialized sorts, and some mathematical manipulations were carried out in the Metro computer facility. Some examples of the specific operations performed were: (1) computation of tables to show length of stay at Richland Village by reason of entry and age of child; (2) daily loads at Richland Village; (3) Juvenile Court case disposition by reason of entry; (4) listings of all family records when one child in family had been a delinquent and when one child had more than one N&D; and (5) such relatively simple things as the numbers of children entering by reason and the numbers of children placed by Juvenile Court in the various places.

A number of manual analyses was conducted, extracting data from the various computer printouts. The results of many of these analyses are shown in the main text of the report. However, we recommend that appropriate computer programs be used to analyze and reduce as much data as possible if an on-going, continuous evaluation effort is initiated. Some of the standard data management software packages currently available should be able with only minor reprogramming to reduce the data and provide the numbers for the evaluation criteria suggested in Chapter III and employed in Chapter IV and VI.

TABLE D-1

JUVENILE COURT CODING SHEET
(For N&D and for Delinquency Petitions)

COLUMN	CODE EXPLANATION (General Note: Z or 99 means not reported)

1　　　　AFDC status
　　　　　　Y = Receiving AFDC support
　　　　　　N = Not receiving AFDC support

2-5　　　I.D. number - family identification
　　　　　All children in a family to have the same I.D. number
　　　　　even if some have different last names from the others.

7-16　　Date of petition.　Year, month, day, hour.

18-19　　Age

21　　　　Sex

23　　　　Race

24　　　　Number of siblings.

25　　　　Agency or person filing petition.

　　　　　　　A = Both parents
　　　　　　　C = Probation Office
　　　　　　　D = Child (self)
　　　　　　　E = Police Department
　　　　　　　F = Mother
　　　　　　　G = Father
　　　　　　　H = School social worker
　　　　　　　I = Juvenile Court
　　　　　　　J = Department of Public Welfare
　　　　　　　K = Foster parents
　　　　　　　L = Relatives
　　　　　　　M = Neighbors (or babysitters)
　　　　　　　Q = Other
　　　　　　　Z = If delinquency petition

27　　　　Reported reason for entry.

　　　　　　　A = Alleged neglect
　　　　　　　B = Alleged abuse
　　　　　　　C = Emotional difficulties of parents or guardians in-
　　　　　　　　　cluding drunkenness of mother
　　　　　　　D = Sickness or hospitalization of parents or guardians

TABLE D-1 (CONTINUED)

COLUMN	CODE EXPLANATION (General Note: Z or 99 means not reported)

27

    E = Incarceration of one or both parents or guardians
    F = Financial difficulties
    G = Marital difficulties of parents
    H = Death of one or both parents
    I = Family unable to find adequate housing
    J = Other
    K = Child's emotional problems
    L = Delinquency of child
    M = Child awaiting disposition to state facilities
    N = Parents or guardians cannot control child
    P = Conflict with parents
    R = Runaway
    S = Divorce proceedings of parents underway
    U = Foster parents or relatives unable to keep child
    V = Requirement for custody
    W = Alleged abandonment
    X = Release of custody
    Z = Unknown

If juvenile has a delinquency record, list it as a separate entry filling in all the columns that are applicable, but for this column use a number code.

    1 = Truancy
    2 = Loitering
    3 = Acts reflecting family or personal emotional instability
    4 = Disorderly conduct
    5 = Auto theft
    6 = Drug abuse
    7 = Alcohol
    8 = Felonious charges
    9 = Other misdemeanor charges

29

Number of previous Neglect and Dependency petitions. Also make a separate entry for each case. If delinquent petition, give number of previous delinquent petitions.

31

Temporary placement prior to court ordered disposition.

    A = None - kept at home
    B = Richland Village
    C = Juvenile Detention Center
    D = DPW temporary home for infants under three
    E = Hospital
    F = Mother
    G = Father
    H = Relatives
    I = Petitioner
    J = Temporary Foster Home

TABLE D-1 (CONTINUED)

COLUMN	CODE EXPLANATION (General Note: Z or 99 means not reported)

31
        K = Others
        Z = Not reported

33
&
35

Probation Office disposition recommendation

DPW disposition recommendation

    A = Both parents
    B = Relatives
    C = Foster home
    D = Police
    E = No recommendation, but report filed
    F = Mother
    G = Father
    H = Voluntary Care Institution
    I = State long-term care institution
    K = Runaway
    S = Self
    W = Case dismissal
    Y = Intensive casework supervision
    Z = Unknown or not included
    2 = Custody to petitioner

37-41
Date of final court hearing, month, day. If case is continued a few days to get additional information, then use date of continuation. If continued a long time as a type of probation, then use date of first court hearing. If case not heard, but dropped without trial being set, list as 99, 99.

43
Juvenile Court disposition.

    A = Both parents
    B = Relatives
    C = Foster home
    D = Police
    E = Continuation
    F = Mother
    G = Father
    H = Voluntary care institution
    I = State long-term care institution
    K = Runaway
    S = Self
    U = Other
    V = Withdrawal of petition, no decision, case not decided, defendants did not appear, no action taken
    W = Informally dismissed
    Y = Intensive casework supervision
    3 = Richland Village
    Z = Unknown

TABLE D-2

DEPARTMENT OF PUBLIC WELFARE CODING SHEET

COLUMN	CODE EXPLANATION (General Note: Z or 99 means not reported)

45   Quality of disposition. This is subjective. Fill out in the following way: if sent back home

A = Probably good
B = Questionable
C = Probably bad

if sent to foster home

D = Children separated from brothers and sisters but did not get along with them well anyway
E = Children kept together
F = Children separated but would have been better if kept together

if sent to other places

Z = not applicable

46-51   Date of foster home placement, year, month, day.

53   Adjustment

A = Reasonably well
B = Questionable
C = Probably bad
Z = Unknown

55-61   Date left or moved from foster home placement, year month, day

62   Destination

A = Both parents
B = Relatives
C = Guardian/custodian
D = Release to self due to "Majority" status
E = Psychiatric institution
F = Mother
G = Father
J = Tennessee Preparatory School
P = State Vocational Training School
U = Other
X = Continued foster home placement
Z = Unknown

TABLE D-2 (CONTINUED)

COLUMN

CODE EXPLANATION (General Note: Z or 99 means not reported)

64   Reason for leaving foster home

        A = Emotional stability of home re-established
        B = Financial stability of home re-established
        C = Secondary family resource located
        F = Institutional care
        J = Delinquency of child
        K = Sickness of child requiring long-term care
        L = Death of child
        M = Foster parents cannot control child
        O = Child better suited for group living than foster care
        P = Emotional difficulties of foster parents
        Q = Sickness or hospitalization of foster parents
        S = Child's emotional problem
        T = Foster parents unable to keep child
        U = Other
        V = Conflict with foster parents
        W = Runaway from foster home
        X = Continued foster care placement
        Y = Youth reached "Majority" status
        Z = Unknown

65   Number of foster home placements

TABLE D-3

BOARD OF EDUCATION CODING SHEET

COLUMN	CODE EXPLANATION
2-5	Family I.D.
7-9	WISC Score
11	Year of WISC Score
13-15	Stanford-Binet Score
17	Year of Stanford-Binet Score
19	Latest PPVT or Otis Score, by IQ range

        A = 0-55
        B = 56-70
        C = 71-85
        D = 86-100
        E = 101-115
        F = Above 115

COLUMN	CODE EXPLANATION
21-22	Grade in school
26-32	Type of handicap--professional opinion of school psychologist or other professional
26	Emotionally disturbed

        Y = Yes
        N = No

COLUMN	CODE EXPLANATION
28	Physical or other handicap (including visual and auditory deficiencies)

        Y = Yes
        N = No

COLUMN	CODE EXPLANATION
30	Mental (intellectual deficiency)

        Y = Yes
        N = No

COLUMN	CODE EXPLANATION
36	Equivalent socio-economic level Taken from a conversion table used by the Board of Education that is based upon ESEA (Elementary Secondary Act) Title I criteria

TABLE D-3 (CONTINUED)

<u>COLUMN</u>   <u>CODE EXPLANATION</u>

                            A = Low
                            B = Low - Low/middle
                            C = Low/middle - Middle
                            D = Low/middle - Upper
                            E = Middle - Upper

66+   Name of client

117

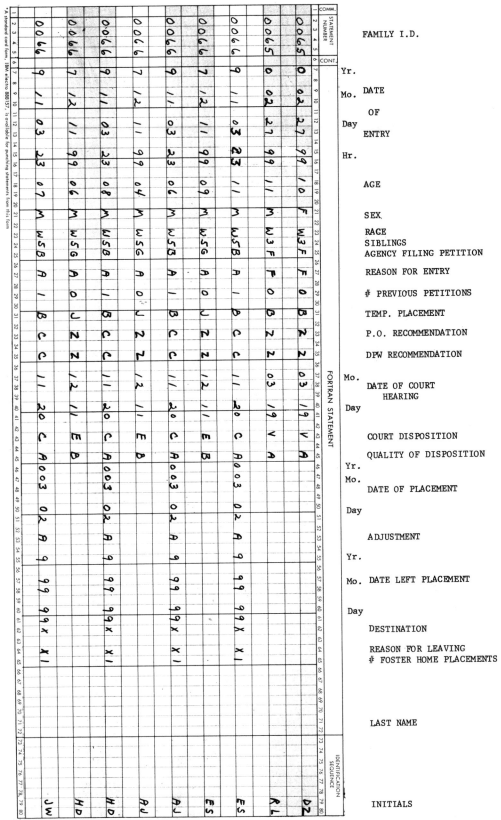

FIGURE D-1 — JUVENILE COURT AND DPW COMBINED RECORDING FORM

APPENDIX E

Richland Village
Cost Analysis

The total fiscal year 1969-70 operating costs at Richland Village were $176,767. The essential question addressed here is how the costs change if the number of children (and, therefore, child-years) are reduced when an alternative N&D system is introduced.

Table E-1 shows the number of children at Richland Village during each month of the period January 1, 1968 through April 20, 1970.[1] The total days of care (child-days), highest and lowest number of children present on any one day, and average number present per day during each month are shown. The "Bed Count" includes only children present overnight (i.e., occupy a bed) and "Case Load" indicates the number of children present at any time during that day. "Bed Count" more nearly reflects the relationship of the number of children to the capacity, as capacity is expressed in terms of beds; "Case Load" is a better cost indicator. The children must be fed, supervised, and administered to whether they remain overnight or not. The differences in average days of care between them is slight, however (less than 2 percent). We will use 57, the average "Case Load" in 1969, as our base figure.

Table E-2 shows the child-years of care at Richland Village that would result under each of the four alternatives analyzed in Chapter IV. For example, if Alternative I were implemented, the child-years would be reduced from 57 to 40 in the first year, and from 57 to 23 in the second.

Staffing

As 73 percent of total costs consist of personnel salaries and benefits, we first consider staffing.

Table E-3 depicts the staffing proposed in the fiscal 1969-1970 budget. As does the entire budget for Richland Village, this table reflects an anticipated average daily load of about 57 children, with daily peaks of up to 84. If we assume that the currently projected staff can handle the current average daily load of about 57 (or about 1,700 days of care per month) we can then examine how staffing and costs vary at the alternative loads in Table E-2. Thus, we consider a reduction in loads up to 34 child-years or 1,020 days of care per month.

---

[1] These data were compiled from daily figures derived from computer processing of the data collected.

120

TABLE E-1

CHILDREN AT RICHLAND VILLAGE — JAN. 1, 1968 — APRIL 20, 1970

Mo./Yr.	Bed Count[a]				Case Load[b]			
	Total[c]	High[d]	Low[e]	Average[f]	Total[c]	High[d]	Low[e]	Average[f]
1968	18,488	81	30	56	18,798	76	30	53
January	2,104	72	60	68	2,141	76	63	69
February	1,826	71	54	63	1,857	71	56	64
March	1,785	63	51	58	1,804	63	52	58
April	1,304	50	37	43	1,331	53	37	44
May	1,138	44	31	37	1,157	45	31	37
June	1,383	53	40	46	1,410	53	40	47
July	1,302	51	30	42	1,334	51	30	43
August	1,461	52	35	47	1,487	53	35	48
September	1,401	63	35	47	1,427	64	35	48
October	1,672	60	50	54	1,695	60	50	55
November	1,665	59	52	56	1,674	59	52	56
December	1,444	61	31	47	1,481	62	31	48
1969	20,316	81	30	56	20,760	84	30	57
January	1,108	44	30	36	1,139	45	30	37
February	1,275	52	36	46	1,296	52	39	46
March	1,294	52	36	42	1,328	53	36	43
April	1,530	63	43	51	1,558	65	45	52
May	2,104	80	59	68	2,145	81	59	69
June	1,988	80	52	66	2,047	81	52	68
July	1,618	61	47	52	1,648	63	48	53
August	1,584	55	47	51	1,602	57	47	52
September	2,013	75	51	67	2,057	77	51	69
October	2,012	76	61	65	2,054	76	61	66
November	2,018	79	59	67	2,082	84	59	69
December	1,772	65	49	57	1,804	67	51	58
1970	6,182	71	36	54	6,327	76	39	58
January	1,911	69	57	62	1,950	73	58	63
February	1,644	71	50	59	1,669	73	52	60
March	1,753	71	43	57	1,811	76	44	58
April[g]	874	54	36	44	897	54	39	45

[a]Children who stay overnight (i.e. occupy beds).
[b]Total children present.
[c]Days of care (child-days).
[d]Highest number of children on one day.
[e]Lowest number of children on one day.
[f]Average number of children per day during the month.
[g]1st - 20th only.

TABLE E-2

CHILD-YEARS OF CARE AT RICHLAND VILLAGE

	Alternative I		Alternative II		Alternative III		Alternative IV	
	1st Year	2nd[c] Year	1st Year	2nd[c] Year	1st Year	2nd[c] Year	1st Year	2nd[c] Year
Average Load								
1969[a]	57	57	57	57	57	57	57	57
Less Reduction[b]	17	34	17	34	10	20	1	1
NEW TOTAL	40	23	40	23	47	37	56	56

[a]Table E-1.

[b]Based on case-weeks of care under each alternative in Chapter IV (Table IV-10).

[c]Also applies to each subsequent year.

TABLE E-3

RICHLAND VILLAGE — STAFF

	Positions	Wages and Salaries	
		Unit Cost	Total
Fixed			
Asst. to sup./soc. worker	1	$ 5,424	5,424
Steno/clerk	1	5,774	5,774
Clinical psychologist (superintendent)	1	11,448	11,448
Subtotal			$ 22,646
Semi-variable			
Maid	4	$ 3,725	$14,899
Cook	3	4,342	13,025
House parent	12	4,451	53,412
Social workers	2	7,965	15,931
			$ 97,267
			$119,913[a]

[a]These represent the budgeted amounts. Actual costs incurred were $114,837 due to turnover in the semi-variable positions--a reduction of $5,076 or 5.2 percent of the semi--variable wage and salaries cost.

Six cottages are now planned in order to maintain appropriate reloca-
tion of children by sex and age; each have a capacity of 15-18 children,
with 18 being on the overcrowded side for a total capacity of 90-108
children.[1] This more than covers even the highest figures shown in Table
E-1 and would substantially exceed the capacity required at the reduced
loads in Table E-2.

Table E-4 shows the estimated semi-variable staffing required at each
of the loads (child-years) shown in Table E-2. At an average load of 23,
it is assumed that only three cottages would be required,[2] four at 37, five
at 40, and six at 56.

Operating Costs

Table E-5 depicts fiscal year 1969-70 operating costs by object class
divided into fixed, semi-variable, and variable. By definition, the fixed
costs do not change at different loads, and variable costs vary in proportion to the loads. The difficult category is semi-variable costs (which
constitute 67 percent of the total costs).

Table E-6 shows the estimated semi-variable costs at average monthly
loads of 23, 37, 40, 47 and 56 children.

Table E-7 shows the total annual operating costs at the five average
loads (average number of children) under consideration. If the load were
reduced from the present 57 to 23, the annual operating costs would be
reduced from the present $176,800 to $102,000 for a savings of $74,800.

Capital costs (e.g., for constructing the cottages and other buildings)
are already expended ("sunk") and nothing in our analysis is likely to have
any effect on them. The metro government is continuing to pay an annual
debt service cost, but this can not be affected by any of our alternatives
considered in this report.

In projecting the operating costs analyzed herein to the 1971-1972
period, they should be inflated by 10 percent consistent with the practice
in Chapters III and IV.

---

[1]Four of these cottages are currently being utilized; an additional
two are under construction and will be occupied early in 1971. Some children are currently housed in a condemned building soon to be demolished.

[2]It could be argued that only two cottages are required at an average
load of 23--this would give a surplus capacity of 13 to handle potential
peak loads (i.e. 56 percent capacity above the average load). This actually
exceeds, on a percentage basis, the peaking in 1969 shown in Table E-1; this
shows a highest load of 81 which is 45 percent above the average of 56. We
are reluctant to cut our estimates so close, however, and some separation
by age and sex is required.

TABLE E-4

RICHLAND VILLAGE STAFFING — SEMI-VARIABLE

| | Average number of children per day | | | | | | | | | |
| | 23 | | 37 | | 40 | | 47 | | 56 | |
	#	$000	#	$000	#	$000	#	$000	#	$000
Maid	2	7.5	3	11.2	3	11.2	4	14.9	4	14.9
Cook	2	8.7	2	8.7	3	13.0	3	13.0	3	13.0
House parents	6	26.7	8	35.6	10	44.5	10	44.5	12	53.4
Social workers	1	8.0	1	8.0	2	15.9	2	15.9	2	15.9
Total	--	50.9	--	63.5	--	84.6	--	88.3	--	97.3[a]
Less turnover (5.2%)	--	2.7	--	3.3	--	4.4	--	4.6	--	5.1
Net	--	48.2	--	60.2	--	80.2	--	83.7	--	92.2

[a]Difference due to rounding.

TABLE E-5

RICHLAND VILLAGE:
COST BY CLASSIFICATION/OBJECT CODE — FISCAL YEAR 1969-70

Object Code No.	Classification	Fixed Cost	Semi-Variable Costs	Variable Costs	Total Costs
111	Salaries	$22,646.00	$ 91,258.95[a]	--	$113,904.95
112	Temporary of P/T Salary		932.30[a]		932.30
	TOTAL WAGES AND SALARIES			--	114,837.25
211	Postage, Bos Rent, etc.		111.00		111.00
216	Radio and T.V. Service		93.30		93.30
213	Publication of formal & Legal Notices		157.44		157.44
238	Employee Expense Reimbursement		49.16		49.16
241	Electric, Light and Power		5,935.70		5,935.70
242	Water		1,405.41		1,405.41
243	Gas		2,883.37		2,883.37
244	Telephone and Telegraph		54.84		54.84
249	Sundry		226.45		226.45
251	Medical, Dental, Veterinary & Vital Statistics Services			$1,031.00	1,031.00
262	Buildings		8.75		8.75
263	Automobiles and Trucks		63.08		63.08
264	Machinery & Equipment		871.54		871.54
266	Furniture, Office Machines & Equipment		137.40		137.40
269	Electrical Services		14.06		14.06
270	Laundry & Sanitation Serv.			924.70	924.70
271	Disinfecting & Pest Control Services	164.00			164.00
276	Inspecting & Testing Pipes and Mains	2.00			2.00
281	Motor Pool			320.00	320.00
282	Employee Auto Allowance			1,298.96	1,298.96
283	Out-of-town Expense			14.30	14.30
291	Subsistence & Care of Persons			2,331.32	2,331.32
292	Educational, Exhibition, Hobby & Recreation Serv.		262.29		262.29
295	Barber & Beauty Services			1,481.89	1,481.89
311	Office Supplies & Stationery		384.41		384.41
314	Food and Ice			16,373.40	16,373.40
315	Household and Occupancy		271.94		271.94
316	Clothing, Bed Linen, Towels,etc.			7,125.30	7,125.30
317	Kitchen and Dining Room		589.72		589.72
319	Drugs and Medicine			296.98	296.98
328	Educational & Scientific			525.16	525.16
329	Electrical Supplies & Light Bulbs		72.28		72.28
330	Laundry, Cleaning and Sanitation			816.46	816.46
334	Gasoline, Oil, etc.		41.40		41.40
336	Repair Parts		414.63		414.63
339	Recreational Supplies			883.33	883.33
342	Plumbing Supplies		205.82		205.82
399	Sundry		25.48		25.48
421	Small Hardware, Wire, Nails		92.58		92.58
321	Farm Supplies		72.78		72.78
	SUB TOTAL	$22,812.00	$106,636.08	$33,422.80	$162,870.88
	Employees Benefits @12.2% of Salaries	2,763.00	11,133.00	--	13,896.00
	TOTAL	$25,595.00	$117,769.08	$33,422.80	$176,766.88

[a] Discussed under "staffing."

TABLE E-6

SEMI-VARIABLE COST ($000)

Code	Object class	Cost at average load--child years				
		23[b]	37[c]	40[d]	47[e]	56[f]
111	Salaries[a]	48.2	60.2	80.2	83.7	92.2
241	Elec. Lt. & Power	4.0	4.6	5.3	5.3	5.9
242	Water	0.7	0.9	1.2	1.2	1.4
243	Gas	2.0	2.3	2.7	2.7	2.9
292	Educ. hobby & exp.	0.1	0.2	0.3	0.3	0.3
315	Household & occup.	0.2	0.2	0.3	0.3	0.3
317	Kitchen & dining room	0.3	0.4	0.5	0.5	0.6
Misc.	All other	1.5	2.0	2.5	2.7	3.0
	Benefits	5.9	7.5	9.1	9.5	11.1
	Total	62.9	78.3	102.1	106.2	117.8[g]

[a]From Table E-4.

[b]Table IV-10, Alternative I or II, 2nd year.

[c]Table IV-10, Alternative III, 2nd year.

[d]Table IV-10, Alternative I or II, 2nd year.

[e]Table IV-10, Alternative III, 1st year.

[f]Table IV-10, Alternative IV, 1st or 2nd year.

[g]Difference due to rounding.

TABLE E-7

METROPOLITAN CHILDRENS HOME
ANNUAL OPERATING COST AT ALTERNATIVE LOADS
($000)

COST CLASSIFICATION	LOAD--Child-years				
	23	37	40	47	56
Fixed[a]	25.6	25.6	25.6	25.6	25.6
Semi-Variable[b]	62.9	78.3	102.1	106.2	117.8
Variable[c]	13.5	21.7	23.4	27.5	32.8
Total	102.0	125.6	151.1	159.3	176.2
Savings[d]	74.8	51.2	25.7	17.5	0.6

[a]From Table E-5.

[b]From Table E-6.

[c]Variable cost $586 per child-year (33,422 ÷ 57) from Table E-5.

[d]Annual operating costs at each load compared to annual operating costs in Table E-5 ($176.8 thousand).

APPENDIX H

Methodology

This analysis utilized a program analysis methodology incompassing the following major steps:

-- Definition of the Problem

-- Determination of Program Objectives and Evaluation Criteria

-- Analysis of Alternative Programs for Meeting the Objectives

Definition of the Problem

The problem of how to improve the current N&D child welfare system was defined through extensive discussions with persons in each element of the system shown in Figure II-1. Specific characteristics and the magnitude of the problem were obtained through the data system described in Appendix D which was used to evaluate the current system. The central task of the study was to identify: the numbers and types of children who enter the system for various reasons, alternative programs to meet their needs, and the projected effectiveness and cost of each alternative program.

Determination of Program Objectives and Evaluation Criteria

The program objectives and evaluation criteria to measure the extent to which the objectives were achieved (discussed in Chapter III) were derived by reviewing the extensive literature relating to the care of N&D children, in light of the problems in Nashville. The major program objectives were: to reduce the number of children entering the system; to keep N&D children in their own homes or in family environments whenever possible; and to reduce the number of children that have to be placed at Richland Village.

It was assumed that in each of the next 5 years the total number of children coming to the attention of the N&D system will be the same as it was for 1969 - specifically 632 children. They will come in for the same types of reasons, have the same needs and be responsive to the same types of care as those who entered in 1969. It was further assumed that the effectiveness of proposed programs will be the same in future years as they would have been had the program been available at that time. Thus the effectiveness of the proposed programs was estimated by determining the number of 1969 N&D children who would have been benefited from such programs. This was accomplished by going through the various classes of cases to determine whether the particular service being proposed would have provided better service for that class than they received under the existing system. Better service was defined, in accordance with the objectives and evaluation criteria in Chapter III, as keeping the child out of the system if he didn't really need to come into it or by keeping him in his own home or a family environment rather than placing him in Richland Village prior to the Juvenile Court hearing. The effectiveness of each program was measured by the total number of children to whom it would have provided better service using the data system discussed in Appendix D to determine in how many cases each type of service would have been appropriate.

For example, it was assumed that all children who were placed at Richland Village for reasons of neglect, or sickness or incarceration of their parents and then returned to their own homes could have been served better by a homemaker service. There were 252 children in this category in 1969 (see Figure IV-2). Then a calculation was made, as shown in Appendix J, to determine how many homemakers would be required to care for any specified number of these children. For example, according to Figure IV-2, 15 homemakers could provide service to 146 children. Thus the effectiveness of a 24-hour a day program with 15 homemakers was 146 children avoiding institutionalization.

Costs were estimated by determining the personnel and facilities required for each program, and escalating current personnel costs by 10% per year to account for inflation. In two cases, comparable programs in other cities were analyzed to arrive at costs for Nashville/Davidson County. First year costs are based on spending 6 months to develop and implement the program and only 6 months of actual program operation. Second year and succeeding year costs are for 12 months operating costs and no program development costs.

Analysis of Alternative Programs for Meeting the Objectives

Four alternative combined programs for short-term care to supplement the current system were proposed and their effectiveness and costs estimated in Chapter IV. Each one represented a different mix of short-term options. They ranged from an essentially unconstrained program designed to provide the best care to all the children to a minimal program providing limited care to only a small portion of the children. The costs to Metro were estimated under AFDC, LEAA, and the proposed FAP funding.

Cost savings at Richland Village were estimated for each of the four alternative programs by breaking the 1969 costs into its fixed, semi-variable, and variable components and making the appropriate calculations for the respective child care load. This cost analysis is shown in Appendix E.

Alternative ways to improve long-term care after the Juvenile Court hearing are discussed in Chapter VI. It was assumed that the number of N&D children requiring foster care will continue to increase at the same rate at which it increased between 1969 and 1970.

A Proposed Child Welfare System for Preventing and Handling Abuse, Dependency, and Neglect Complaints

Figure I-1 shows a suggested child welfare system aimed at prevention and handling of abuse, dependency, and neglect complaints. It was developed by Beatrice Garrett, Specialist in Foster Family Care, Office of Child Development, Department of Health, Education and Welfare. It depicts a system toward which Nashville could consider moving.

In the event of an incident, all complaints would be referred to the Department of Public Welfare. These complaints may originate from an individual, a consultation team that has "found" cases, or possibly a 24-hour neighborhood part-time child care center. If the complaint occurs after working hours, the emergency intake answering service would refer the case either to other community resources or to an emergency social worker. The emergency social worker would then refer the children to an emergency caretaker, a homemaker, an emergency foster home, or to a family shelter.[1] The emergency social worker would then report at the beginning of the next working day to the DPW outreach intake unit.

All incidents during working hours would be referred directly to the outreach intake unit. The DPW outreach intake unit may offer social services to the family which may or may not be accepted. If the offer is accepted, ordinarily no petition would be recommended by the DPW for filing in Juvenile Court. In this case, some children would be placed voluntarily in a temporary foster family home, a group home, or a treatment institution.

If a complainant petitions Juvenile Court, the DPW would study the case and make a recommendation to Juvenile Court for disposition; or the agency may itself petition Juvenile Court and make a recommendation. The Juvenile Court would hold a hearing within one week after a petition is filed. The judge must then decide whether to: (1) dismiss the case, (2) require DPW intensive supervision in the child's own home, or (3) award custody elsewhere. In the event of intensive supervision, a report must be submitted to the Juvenile Court by the DPW within six months. Custody of the children may be awarded to the DPW or to a voluntary agency. In either case, a report must be filed by the agency with the Juvenile Court within one year.

Another possible outcome of the hearing could be that social services are provided to the family. The role of Richland Village in this model would be primarily as a treatment institution to include treatment of both in-patients and out-patients. The out-patients treated would probably be children in foster care, with involvement of the foster parents. For

---

[1]The family shelter could be some type of apartment unit wherein the whole family may be maintained.

children placed in foster family care, group homes, or treatment institutions, several options would be pursued:

1. The first attempt would be to return the child to an approved home within one or two years; or

2. voluntary relinquishment or court termination of parental rights for adoption and placement (within one year of original placement);[1] or

3. placement in a permanent foster family home; or

4. permanent placement in a group facility.

---

[1]A subsidized adoption program is essential for this to succeed.

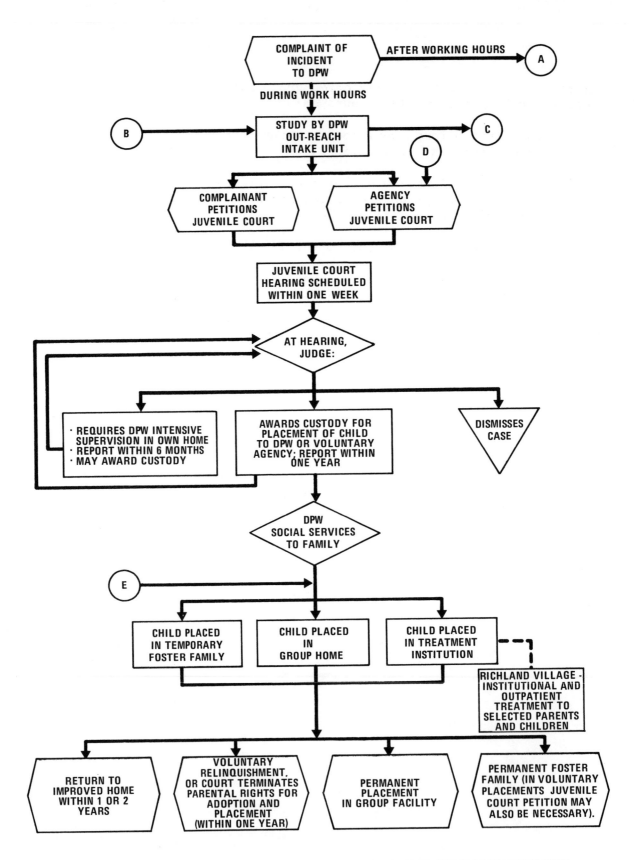

FIGURE I-1. CHILD WELFARE SYSTEM FOR HANDLING ABUSE, DEPENDENCY, AND NEGLECT COMPLAINTS

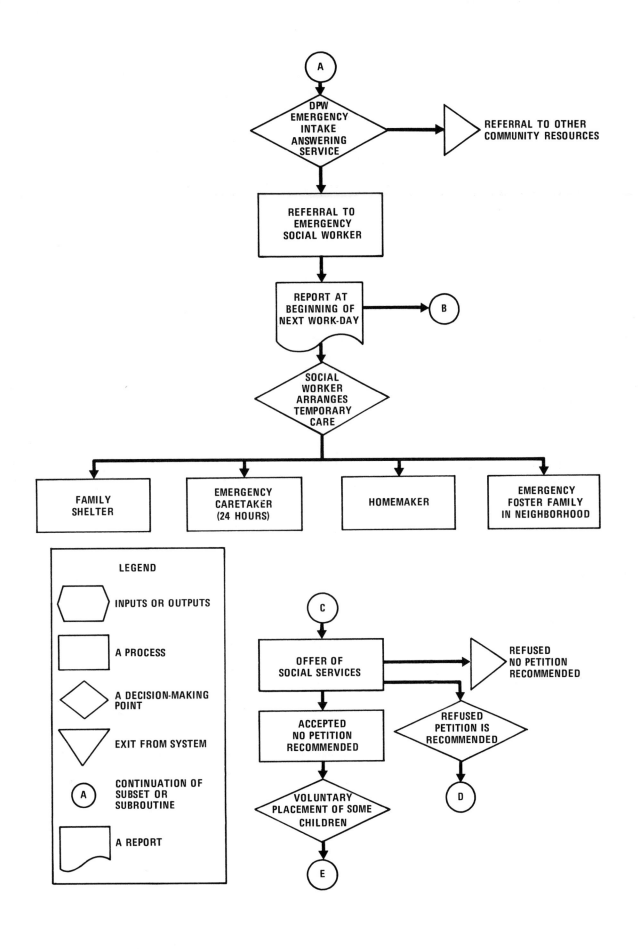

A

DPW
EMERGENCY
INTAKE
ANSWERING
SERVICE → REFERRAL TO OTHER
COMMUNITY RESOURCES

REFERRAL TO
EMERGENCY
SOCIAL WORKER

REPORT AT
BEGINNING OF
NEXT WORK-DAY → B

SOCIAL
WORKER
ARRANGES
TEMPORARY
CARE

FAMILY
SHELTER

EMERGENCY
CARETAKER
(24 HOURS)

HOMEMAKER

EMERGENCY
FOSTER FAMILY
IN NEIGHBORHOOD

LEGEND

INPUTS OR OUTPUTS

A PROCESS

A DECISION-MAKING
POINT

EXIT FROM SYSTEM

A CONTINUATION OF
SUBSET OR
SUBROUTINE

A REPORT

C

OFFER OF
SOCIAL SERVICES → REFUSED
NO PETITION
RECOMMENDED

ACCEPTED
NO PETITION
RECOMMENDED

REFUSED
PETITION IS
RECOMMENDED

VOLUNTARY
PLACEMENT OF SOME
CHILDREN

E

D

APPENDIX J

Calculation of Homemaker Requirements

The method of calculating the number of homemakers required to maintain children in their own homes is illustrated in this example which uses some of the actual data during April to September 1969. Figure IV-2 in the main text was derived by using these techniques on all the cases that arose during 1969. The exact same computation calculates the number of foster homes required if each neglected family is placed in a separate foster home rather than placing a homemaker in the home.

A Gant-Chart, a five-month portion of which is shown in Figure J-1, was plotted showing the date of entry and length of stay for these children. The homemakers were allocated in the following way. The first homemaker, indicated by the letter "A," was assigned to the first case and stayed with it until it ended. Then she was assigned to the next available case, and so on, throughout the 4-month period during which she had a total of five family cases. The second homemaker, indicated by the letter "B," was assigned to the second case coming in and stayed with it until it ended. She was assigned to the next available case, assuming that the first homemaker had not been assigned it. The rest of the homemakers were assigned in similar fashion until all of the family cases had been served by homemakers. Figure J-2 was then plotted to show the number of families served by various levels of homemakers. From this example it would seem relatively uneconomical to provide more than eight 8-hour homemakers or sixteen 24-hour homemakers.

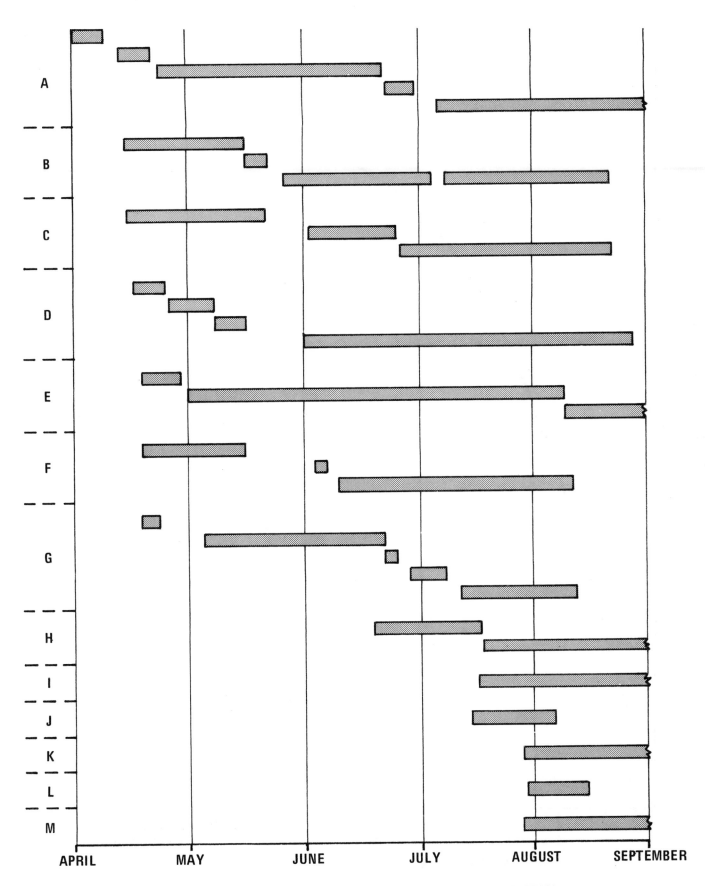

FIGURE J-1. DATE OF ENTRY AND LENGTH OF STAY OF FAMILY
CASES AT RICHLAND VILLAGE ILLUSTRATIVE EXAMPLE
(LETTERS REFER TO HOMEMAKER ASSIGNED TO CASE)

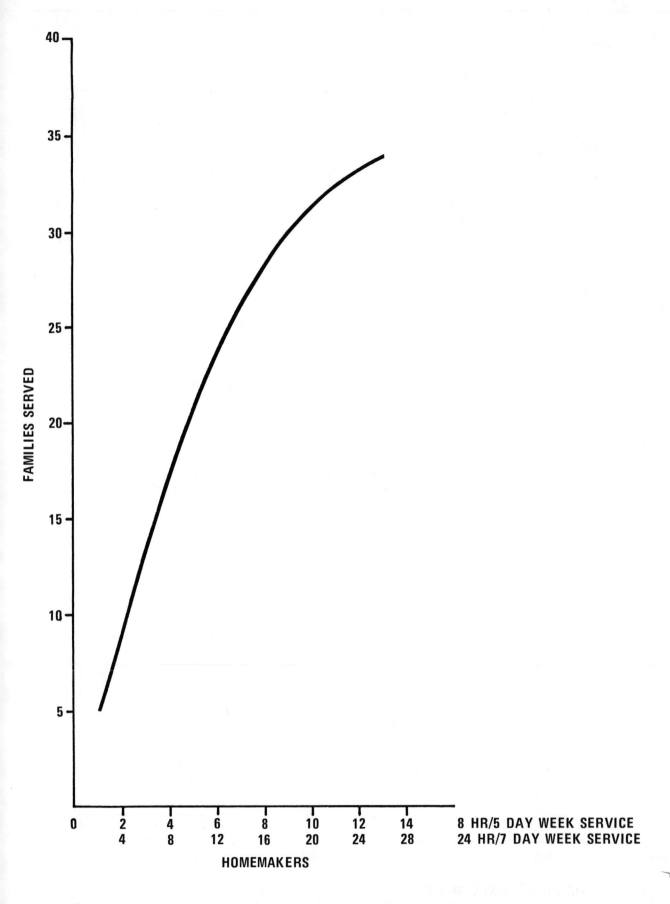

40

35

30

25

FAMILIES SERVED

20

15

10

5

0   2   4   6   8   10   12   14   8 HR/5 DAY WEEK SERVICE
    4   8   12   16   20   24   28   24 HR/7 DAY WEEK SERVICE

HOMEMAKERS

 FIGURE J-2. NUMBER OF FAMILIES SERVED BY HOMEMAKERS, ILLUSTRATIVE EXAMPLE